Larousse
THE WORLD WE LIVE IN

Text by Simone Lamblin

Illustration by Christian Bessière

Adaptation by Howard E. Smith, Jr.

Larousse & Company, Inc./New York, New York

English translation and adaptation © 1982 by Librairie Larousse, U.S.A., Inc.
MA PREMIERE ENCYCLOPEDIE © 1982 by Librairie Larousse, S.A., Paris

All rights reserved. Printed in the United States of America
No part of this publication may be reproduced, stored in a retrieval system,
or transmitted in any form or by any means, electronic or mechanical, photocopying,
recording or otherwise, without the prior written permission of the publisher.

Library of Congress Cataloging in Publication Data

Smith, Howard Everett, Jr. 1927–
 Larousse the world we live in.

 Adaptation of: Ma première encyclopédie/Simone
Lamblin.
 Includes index.
 Summary: Introduces basic concepts about nature,
the human body, and social activities of people.
 1. Natural history—Juvenile literature.
2. Human biology—Juvenile literature. 3. Human
behavior—Juvenile literature. [1. Natural history.
2. Body, Human. 3. Social sciences] I. Lamblin,
Simone. II. Bessière, Christian, ill.
III. Lamblin, Simone. Ma première encyclopédie.
IV. Title.
QH48.S6414 1982   031'.02   82-81527
ISBN 0-88332-285-4

Design by Jacques Chazaud
Cover by Christian Bessière
Translation by Susan Wald
Composition by Rockland Typographical Services, Inc.
Printed by Universal Printing Co.

Contents

PART ONE:
THE WORLD OF NATURE   **8**

From Sun to Atom   10

The Life of a Plant   12

Trees, the Largest Plants   14

A Million Animals   16

Animal Habitats   18

Humans and Nature   20

The Changing Earth   22

The Solar System   24

The Atmosphere and Weather   26

Rivers and Seas   28

Ships and Their Ports   30

Hot and Cold   32

PART TWO:
INSIDE THE HUMAN BODY   **34**

The Skeleton and Muscles   36

Our Senses   38

Our Bodies' Defenses   40

Reproduction   42

PART THREE:
PEOPLE AND SOCIETY   **44**

Shelters   46

A Day in the City   48

Energy and How We Use It   50

Machines and Computers   52

Science in Our Lives   54

The Arts   56

Recreation   58

Communications   60

Transportation   62

The World of Tomorrow   64

Index   66

Part One: The World of Nature

We live in a beautiful world. All around us we see the sky and clouds, seas and rivers, and many plants and animals. This is the world of nature. We humans are part of this world. We share the natural environment with many other living things.

In order for living things to grow and develop, the environment must provide what they need. Plants need sunlight, water, air and soil to grow in. Animals and humans must have a place to live, food to eat, air to breathe, and water to drink. We need the sun for its light and warmth.

In nature, all plants and animals depend upon each other. For example, bees and flowers need each other. As a bee gets nectar for honey from a flower, it carries pollen to other flowers, helping the plants to reproduce.

Ecology is the study of how plants and animals, and humans, depend on their environment and on other plants and animals. It also describes how we change the environment, for better or for worse.

All living things, even the smallest, have a role to play in the environment. Tiny insects eat dead things and keep the environment clean. They also serve as food for many types of animals.

Nature is balanced because as old things die, new ones are being born to take their place. There is always about the same number of plants and animals on earth, and this has been true for millions of years.

From Sun to Atom

All living things depend on the sun. It gives us warmth and light.

The leaves of plants make their food with the help of sunlight.

The sun also gives us energy, for coal and oil come from prehistoric plants and tiny animals which stored up energy from the sun as they grew.

The Life Cycle

The leaves of plants use sunlight, carbon dioxide (a gas in the air), water, and nutrients (chemicals) in the soil to make food. Plants give off oxygen, which humans and animals breathe.

Humans and animals exhale carbon dioxide, which plants use.

Plants are eaten by humans and by animals we eat. Then our wastes enrich the soil to "feed" new plants.

Plants and animals trade many substances back and forth, changing them in the process.

This constant changing of one thing into another is called the life cycle.

Elements

Elements are the basic materials of which all living and nonliving things are made. Iron, oxygen, and carbon are among the 105 known elements on earth.

Carbon is the element most important to living things. It combines with other elements to form chemicals needed for life. Plants get carbon from carbon dioxide. Humans and animals get carbon from food.

Hydrogen, the lightest element, is the most common in the universe. The sun is made mostly of hydrogen.

Heavier elements (iron, sulfur, etc.) are often pushed up by volcanoes.

10

Atoms

atom

An atom's core contains a nucleus. Inside the nucleus are protons and neutrons; spinning around the nucleus are electrons. The number of protons, neutrons, and electrons is different for each element.

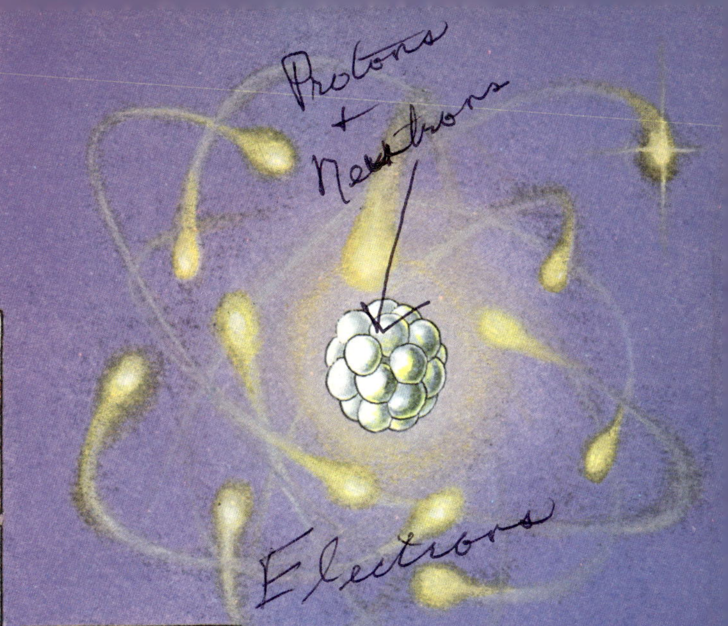

Each element is made up of one kind of atom. An atom is the smallest building block of nature. It is too small to see, even with a powerful microscope. Yet it is not the smallest thing we know of, for it is made of even smaller parts.

molecules

Elements combine to make molecules. All matter consists either of an element or of a molecule made of one or more elements.

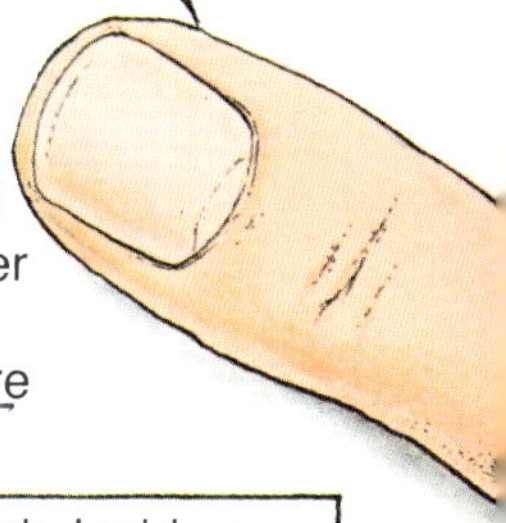

To make molecules, atoms fit together, somewhat like pieces of a jigsaw puzzle. There are thousands of types of molecules.

A simple molecule is water. It is made of two hydrogen atoms and an oxygen atom. Chemists call it H_2O. Carbon dioxide is made of one oxygen atom and two carbon atoms, so it is CO_2. Dextrose sugar is more complicated. It is $C_6H_{12}O_6$.

Our skin is made of countless cells. Each cell represents a huge number of molecules. The atoms within these molecules are in constant motion.

cells

Two or more molecules can react and make a third molecule. To do so, they shift atoms about and trade them.

The Living Cell

Every living being starts life as a single cell in an egg or seed. It is so tiny we need a microscope to see it.

Some adult plants and animals, such as bacteria and protozoans, are composed of just one cell.

In most plants and animals, the single cell in the egg or seed is fertilized by pollen or sperm. Then it divides into two cells, which keep multiplying until the plant or animal is mature.

cells

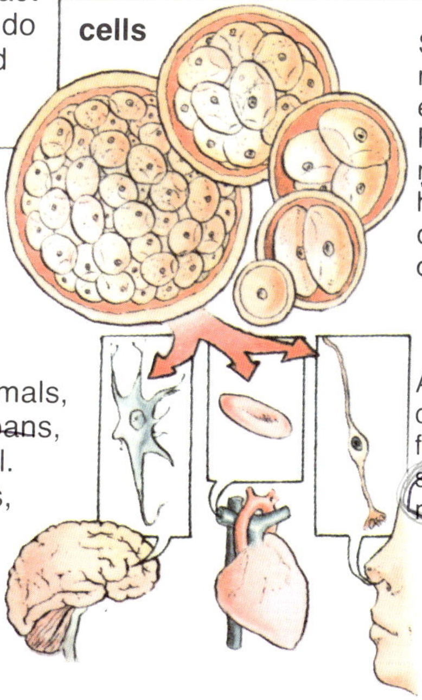

Some living beings have many millions of cells and each has its own job to do. For example, our blood has red corpuscles; the brain has long neuron cells. We detect odors with the help of olfactory cells.

All the time we produce new cells so that our bodies function correctly. In one second we make about 10 million red blood cells!

A cell is like a sack. Inside are life-giving fluids. In the center is the nucleus, which controls the cell's reproduction.

Cells are the smallest units of life. They are what all plants and animals are made of. In fact, plant and animal cells look very much alike.

11

The Life of a Plant

Plants, like all living beings, are made up of cells. Plants reproduce themselves and manufacture their own food.

Flowers have a ring of petals, which are often brightly colored. The female pistil receives the male pollen from the anthers. The anthers are supported by filaments.

So that seeds can be fertilized, pollen must get onto the pistil. Wind may blow it there, or it may be carried by insects. Once on top of the pistil, the grain of pollen forms a tiny living thread that reaches down to the ovary. It unites with the ovule, fertilizing it. It will become a future seed.

Liquid sap carries water from the roots to the rest of the plant; it also carries food made by the leaves to the stem and roots. It moves through sapwood just under the bark of the stem.

Leaves take in CO_2 and give off oxygen.

The bright colors of flowers are useful. They attract insects, which feed on flowers' sweet nectar.

Insects get sticky, powdery pollen on them. They carry it from flower to flower, whose ovules will become fertilized by it.

After fertilization, the flower wilts, and the ovary enlarges and becomes a fruit. The seeds inside will dry and be ready to fall onto the ground.

When a seed gets into the right soil, it will grow. First a small root will grow into the soil. Later a cotyledon, which is a stem with leaves, will sprout above ground.

The cotyledon has food for the new plant until it can make its own.

12

Many plants are grown to feed human beings and livestock. We eat roots (carrots, radishes), leaves (spinach, lettuce), stems (celery, rhubarb), tubers (potatoes), fruit (tomatoes), and the fruits and seeds of podded plants (peas and beans).

Small plants, trees and shrubs give us all kinds of fruit.

Herbs and spices, such as thyme, mint, pepper, add flavors to our foods.

Medicinal plants cure certain illnesses and keep us healthy.

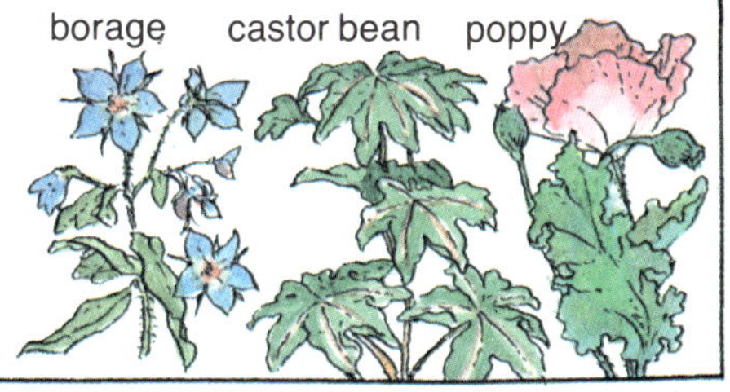

We take oil from the olive tree's fruit and coffee from the seeds (beans) of coffee plants.

Fabrics are made from jute, flax, and cotton.

Meadow hay feeds livestock.

Cereals, such as wheat, rice, corn, and millet are important foods for most people on earth.

Through selective breeding farmers and agricultural experts have transformed many wild plants into hardier, better types of plants more useful to human beings.

Seeds are scattered in many ways. Some are blown in the wind. Some just fall. Some are carried by birds. Some, like coconuts, float in seas. Others stick to fur or wool.

Some plants, called annuals, die in the autumn. Others, perennials, can live through the winter on stored food. They bloom again in the spring.

The food is stored in a potato's tubers; an onion's bulb; the rhizomes of an iris; and the root of a carrot.

Trees, the Largest Plants

Trees are the largest plants. Some are the oldest of all living beings. The bristle-cone pine is over 4,000 years old.

In a forest, everything is constantly renewed. Old logs are eaten by termites. Dead leaves provide fertilizer for new trees.

In the shelter of trees grow shrubs, flowers, ferns, mosses and mushrooms. Birds build nests in branches; small animals live in tree trunks and under large roots.

Trees are valuable. They produce wood, turpentine, and cork. All over the world, valuable trees are grown for fruits: oranges, apples, etc. They also provide us with nuts: almonds, walnuts, coconuts, etc.

Trees help prevent floods, for their roots take up water and hold down the soil. Forests provide vacationers with needed recreational areas for hiking and camping.

As trees make new wood each year, they form rings inside the trunk. By counting rings, we can tell how old a tree is. The trunk grows outward. The new wood of the year is just under the bark. This wood is called cambium or sapwood. Sap goes up and down in tiny tubes inside the wood. In the winter, no sap rises in most trees. But in the spring it starts rising once more. In early spring, the sap of maple trees is gathered to make maple syrup and sugar.

Leaves come in many sizes and shapes. Some are long and thin. Others are wide and round. Some, like pine needles, are sharp and hard. Some, like catalpa, are soft and limp. A few have thorns.

In the spring, buds swell on branches. New leaves or flowers will push out of them.

The bark of a tree protects it in many ways. It holds in needed moisture and protects the tree from infections and rot.

Trees grow so tall— some over 300 feet high —that they need all the support they can get. So large roots hold them up and keep them from falling in the wind.

Trees grow tall so they can get their leaves above other plants where there will be more sunlight.

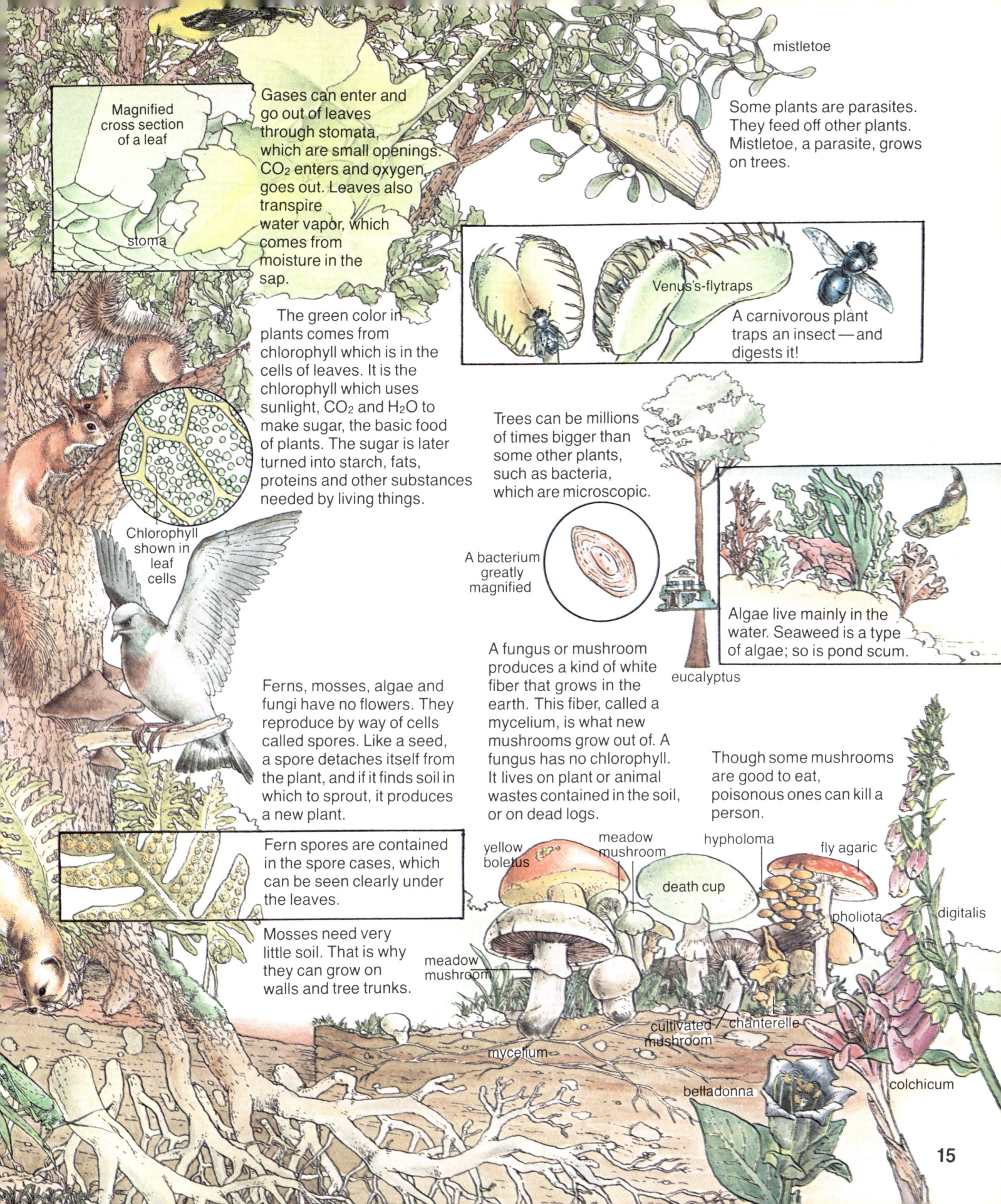

A Million Animals

There are about one million animal species on earth. They range in size from one-celled animals such as amoebas, which are microscopic, to blue whales which are over 100 feet long and weigh 200 tons.

All animals eat food, take in oxygen, and reproduce themselves. They also sense pleasure and pain in varying degrees.

Some animals, such as leopards, live solitary lives except for mating. Others live in large herds (zebras), flocks (birds), or schools (fish).

Herbivores eat only plants, carnivores only meat, and omnivores both meat and plants.

All vertebrate animals (fish, amphibians, reptiles, birds, and mammals) have backbones. Their skeletons are made up of many bones.

Fish are built for swimming. Their bodies are pushed through the water by fins and muscles and their flexible backbones which wiggle. Fish draw oxygen, needed for life, from the water through their gills.

Snails, earthworms, flies, shrimp, and spiders have neither a backbone nor inner skeleton to support their bodies. They are invertebrates. Shellfish and mollusks have hard, outer shells for protection. Insects have tough outer skeletons for support.

Aside from one-celled animals, insects are the most common land animals. There are about 200,000 insect species.

All insects have six legs, a body divided into three parts, and antennae.

The three parts of an insect

An arachnid is not an insect. It has eight legs and its eyes are not like those of an insect.

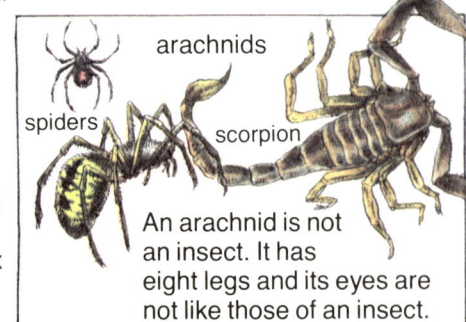

All animals reproduce. Males and females of the same species find each other and mate. Male sperm fertilizes one or more eggs. Once the egg develops there will be new young. Some animals, such as blue whales, have one baby a year, but sea urchins lay millions of eggs.

Mammal young develop inside wombs. When born, they feed on mothers' milk. Marsupial mammals raise their young in pouches on their bodies. A typical marsupial is a kangaroo.

Most animals lay eggs. In a bird's egg, the embryo (the unborn chick) develops until ready to hatch.

Most insects go through life stages. Take a butterfly, for example. When the egg hatches a larva or caterpillar emerges. It spends weeks eating. Then it makes a cocoon. Inside, it remains as a pupa or chrysalis. A butterfly forms and emerges. It is then an adult. It flies off in search of food. Unlike a caterpillar, the butterfly can mate and lay eggs.

Frogs undergo a change, called metamorphosis. First, tadpoles emerge from eggs and live in water. Then they lose their tails and legs grow; they move on land. Later, adult frogs return to water to lay their eggs.

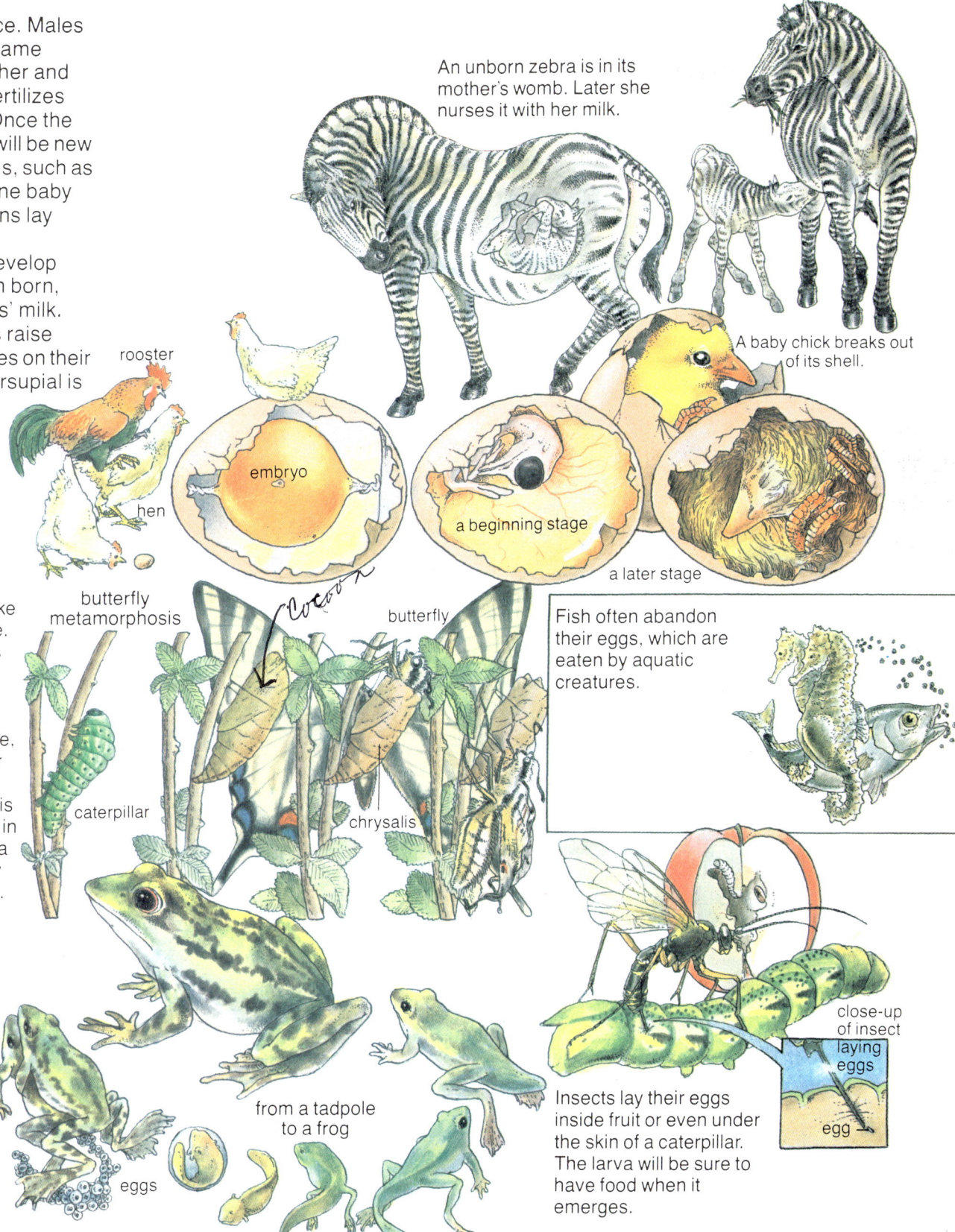

An unborn zebra is in its mother's womb. Later she nurses it with her milk.

A baby chick breaks out of its shell.

Fish often abandon their eggs, which are eaten by aquatic creatures.

Insects lay their eggs inside fruit or even under the skin of a caterpillar. The larva will be sure to have food when it emerges.

from a tadpole to a frog

17

Animal Habitats

All animals need a place to live and grow. Such a place is their habitat. It is where the climate is right and the animals can find food. They will also find places to hide and to make a home.

Animals often mark off places for their own use, called territories. They may keep animals of their own species away from it. They warn them with calls or they may attack invaders.

Deer families herd together in large territories. Others, such as bees, make homes in hives and have organized colonies in a small territory. Thousands of bees live and work together in a hive.
 The queen bee lays eggs after mating with a drone (male bee). Workers gather nectar for honey and do all the other work.

Animals must defend themselves. Moles and hamsters do so by burrowing underground to escape enemies.

Tigers have fangs, rhinoceroses have horns, and crayfish have pincers. Animals are equipped to feed themselves. Birds have different kinds of beaks depending on what they eat. Eagles have hooked beaks for tearing meat; woodpeckers have long ones to hunt for insects; wrens' beaks are shorter for quickly snapping up insects on leaves.

Some animals are protected in other ways. A turtle has its hard shell, a porcupine its needles, a crocodile its tough, scaly skin, and a rhinoceros its thick hide.
 Deer run away when frightened. Pheasants can hide or quickly fly away.

Some animals are difficult for enemies to see. The chameleon can change its colors to match sand or leaves. Note the insects that look so much like leaves, thorns and sticks.

18

In the late autumn many animals go to sleep for the winter. This deep sleep is called hibernation. To keep warm while hibernating, bears, woodchucks, dormice lie in deep holes. Bats hang by their toes in caves.

To escape the cold of winter, swallows, ducks and other birds, and some animals migrate southward to warmer places.

Locusts swarm when there are too many for their territory. They fly off to seek a new place. On the way, they ruin crops.

Salmon return to the territory where they hatched from eggs, so they can lay their own eggs. As they swim upstream, they must leap over waterfalls.

Whales, sea turtles, and ospreys travel long distances to nesting places in old territories. Cheetahs roam to new territories.

19

Humans and Nature

Nature existed long before humans. The first humans stood upright and lived in a natural way by gathering roots, fruits and berries to eat. They did not shape stones into tools or change or control nature.

Later groups of humans began to learn how to control nature. They made tools to plant and gather food and weapons to hunt animals; they learned to use fire for warmth and cooking, to raise animals and build shelters.

Today we are still extending control over nature. We mine the riches of the earth, explore the sea, cut forests, build cities, run farms, operate huge factories. We must do all of this, for we can no longer live in nature as did early humans.

We transform nature, turning crude oil into gasoline, plants into medicines and wool into yarn.

Humans have not only explored the world to find new resources, but we have begun to explore the moon and planets. Humans are always looking for new ways to understand and use nature.

People build cities, factories, dams, and set off atomic explosions. Each affects the environment in some way, either for good or for bad.

People are becoming much more careful not to harm the environment. To prevent damage from occurring, nuclear plants, air pollution, and chemical products are controlled.

More and more, people are trying to protect the environment of our beautiful world.

The Changing Earth

On a clear night, you can see a pale, white river of light across the sky. This is called the Milky Way. This light is made up of hundreds of millions of stars. When you look at the Milky Way, you are looking into our own galaxy. It is disk-shaped and slowly spinning. It rotates every 200 million years. We are near the edge of the disk.

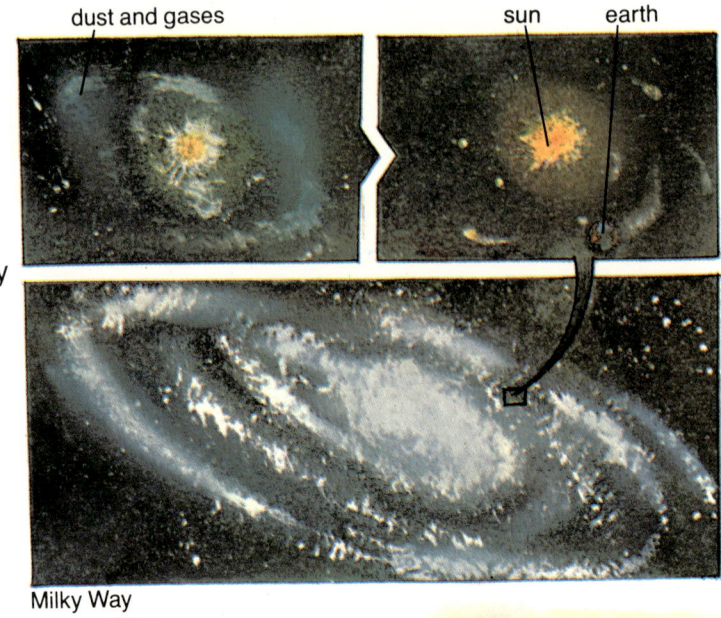

In the Milky Way are vast clouds of dust and gases formed from stars that died long ago. New stars and planets are born of the dust and gases. The top two pictures show the solar system forming out of dust. In the right picture the sun and earth have been formed from the clouds of dust shown in the picture to the left.

Today some dust is left in the solar system. It forms meteors. There are also a few, rare boulders that form meteorites which strike the ground. They are the oldest rocks that scientists have investigated. Some are as old as the earth, about 4.6 billion years old.

The earth is made up of several layers. In the middle of the earth is a core of molten iron. Surrounding the core is a mantle. The rocky material of the mantle is so hot and under such pressure from rocks above that the material slowly bends and stretches. Above the mantle is the crust, made mostly of basalt and granite. As the rocky mantle moves, it pushes continents about. Sometimes the core breaks and hot magma from the mantle rises and forms volcanoes.

Much of the surface of the earth consists of built-up lava from volcanoes which no longer erupt.

Other layers of rock may be formed by other means. Limestone is formed from old sea shells; sandstone from beach sand; shale from muds.

When red-hot magma rises from deep in the earth, volcanoes are formed. Some erupt with great explosions, spewing hot gases and ashes skyward. At other times, molten lava flows down the mountain side. Most volcanoes are cone-shaped. They have craters at their top. Note the crater to the left.

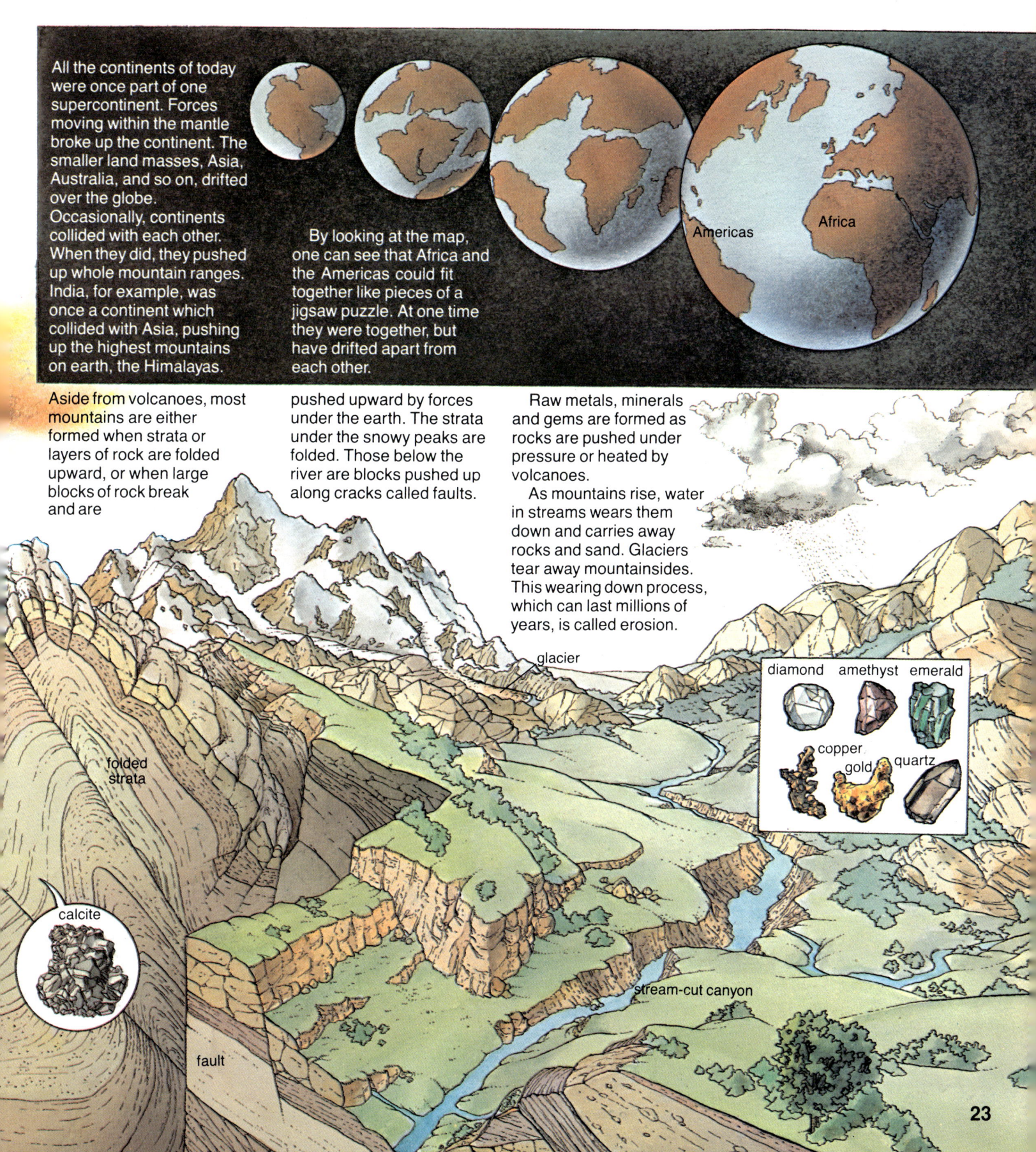

All the continents of today were once part of one supercontinent. Forces moving within the mantle broke up the continent. The smaller land masses, Asia, Australia, and so on, drifted over the globe. Occasionally, continents collided with each other. When they did, they pushed up whole mountain ranges. India, for example, was once a continent which collided with Asia, pushing up the highest mountains on earth, the Himalayas.

By looking at the map, one can see that Africa and the Americas could fit together like pieces of a jigsaw puzzle. At one time they were together, but have drifted apart from each other.

Aside from volcanoes, most mountains are either formed when strata or layers of rock are folded upward, or when large blocks of rock break and are pushed upward by forces under the earth. The strata under the snowy peaks are folded. Those below the river are blocks pushed up along cracks called faults.

Raw metals, minerals and gems are formed as rocks are pushed under pressure or heated by volcanoes.

As mountains rise, water in streams wears them down and carries away rocks and sand. Glaciers tear away mountainsides. This wearing down process, which can last millions of years, is called erosion.

23

The Solar System

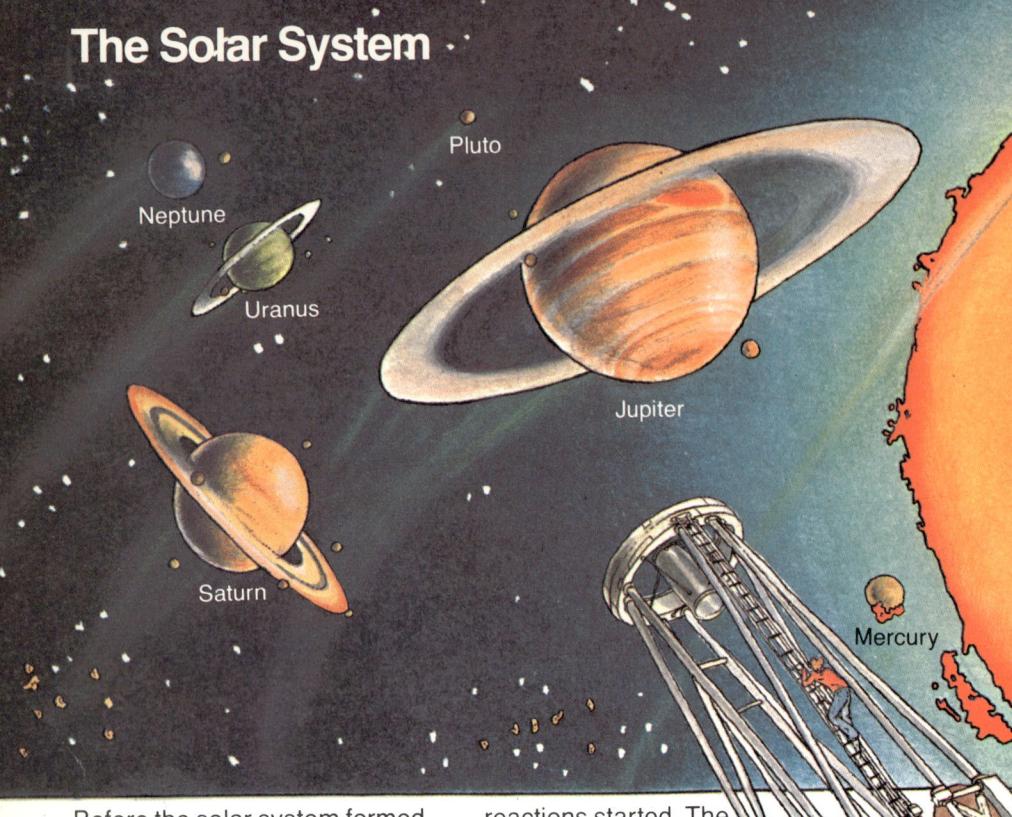

The solar system is a family of heavenly bodies, namely, the sun; nine planets (including Earth); their satellites and asteroids; comets and meteors. The sun is at the center of the solar system, and all the other heavenly bodies orbit around it. The solar system is at least 5.6 trillion miles in diameter.

The sun, which is a medium-sized star, contains 99% of the mass of the solar system. Its surface temperature is 10,000°F. The earth is just far enough from the sun to be neither too hot nor too cold.

At various distances from the sun are the planets Mercury, Venus, Earth, Mars, Jupiter, Saturn, Uranus, Neptune and Pluto. Farther out is a huge number of comets.

Before the solar system formed, large stars blew up. These super-novas scattered gases and dust into space. Millions of years later, gravity pulled the dust and gases together. They formed the sun and planets. The sun became so heavy and grew so hot that atomic reactions started. The planets never became heavy enough to trigger atomic reactions.

Giant telescopes help astronomers learn about the sun, planets, and distant stars.

Because of the super-nova explosions, we can say everything on earth came from the stars. We are made of "star stuff."

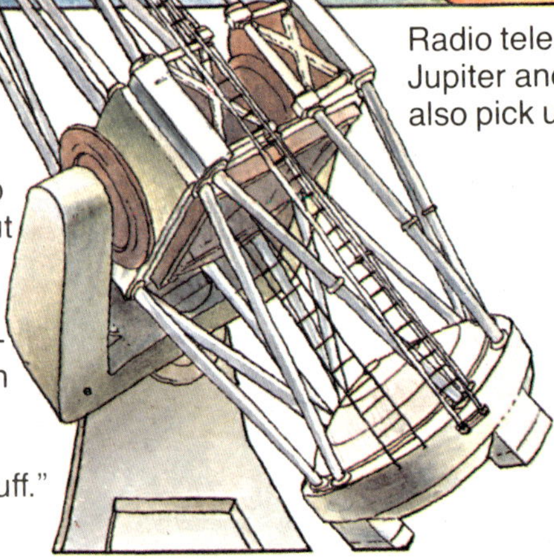

Radio telescopes pick up radio signals from Jupiter and Saturn and the stars. They also pick up signals from distant spacecraft.

Men have landed on the moon and will no doubt go to Mars and other planets. Many instruments, some of which take photographs, have landed on Venus and Mars. Probes with instruments have studied and photographed other planets as they flew by.

Recently, great discoveries about the solar system have been made, for example, the volcanoes of Io, a satellite of Jupiter; the world of Titan, a satellite of Saturn, where there may be life-making chemicals; and much more.

24

There are over a billion billion stars in the part of the universe seen by telescopes. All are far away. Astronomers measure distances to stars in light years. Light travels at 186,282 miles per second in one year. That is about 6 trillion miles. Some stars are 8 billion light years away, but the closest, Alpha Centauri, is 4.28 light years away.

Stars are found in groups called galaxies. There may be a billion stars in one galaxy. There are at least a billion galaxies. Most galaxies are disk-shaped and rotate. New stars form within them from the dust and gases of old stars. Our galaxy is the Milky Way.

The earth orbits the sun once a year (365¼ days). It also spins like a top rotating every 24 hours. At the same time that the earth orbits the sun, the moon orbits the earth, taking 27⅓ days to go around the earth.

Because the earth is round, it can get light from the sun only on one side at a time. As the earth spins, one side and then the other becomes lit, so there is a constant change of days and nights, one after the other.

Because of this, the sun is always rising someplace on earth. But someplace else the sun will be at its highest. It will be noon there. It is a different time everywhere. When it is 7 A.M. in New York, it is 12 noon in Paris. To help people keep time, the earth is divided into 24 time zones.

full moon   crescent moon

Our moon has no light of its own. What we see is the light of the sun reflected from its surface.

For us, because we are on the earth, the moon appears to change its shape from full to crescent to new. These changes are the phases of the moon.

When the moon is between the earth and the sun, it is new and unseen. As it moves in its orbit, it seems to move away from the sun and becomes crescent. When the earth is between the sun and the moon, the moon is full.

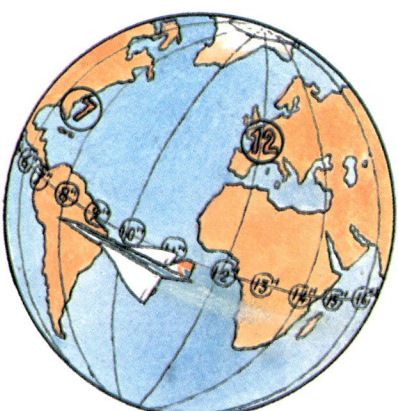

25

The Atmosphere and Weather

The atmosphere surrounds the earth. Also called the air, it contains the gases nitrogen, oxygen and carbon dioxide as well as water vapor.

Near the surface of the earth the air is heavy, but at higher elevations it is less heavy. 99% of the air is found within 20 miles of the surface of the earth. Some air can be found 400 miles high.

Most clouds are below 10 miles high. Meteors start burning up at about 50 miles high. Northern lights occur from 55 to 600 miles high.

Scientists explore the air with various airplanes, high-flying balloons, weather satellites and space probes.

The top picture shows the earth with white clouds moving in the air over blue oceans and brown continents.

The earth has always had an atmosphere, but it has slowly changed. It is not as dense as it was millions of years ago. Thanks to plants, which give off oxygen, there is more oxygen in it today for us and other animals to breathe. The atmosphere protects us from the sun's harmful rays. Winds mix the air so that it is not too hot or too cold anywhere on earth.

Near the poles of the earth the air is cold, but near the equator it is hot. The cold air is much heavier than the warm air. As the cold air comes from the poles it sinks down. At the same time warm air rises near the equator. The air circulates all the time as shown by the arrows, which are red for warm air and blue for cold.

Meteorologists, scientists who study the weather, need instruments. A thermometer tells the temperature. A barometer indicates air pressure. A hygrometer measures the humidity or dampness of the air. A weather vane tells the wind's direction. An anemometer, which the wind rotates, gives the wind's speed.

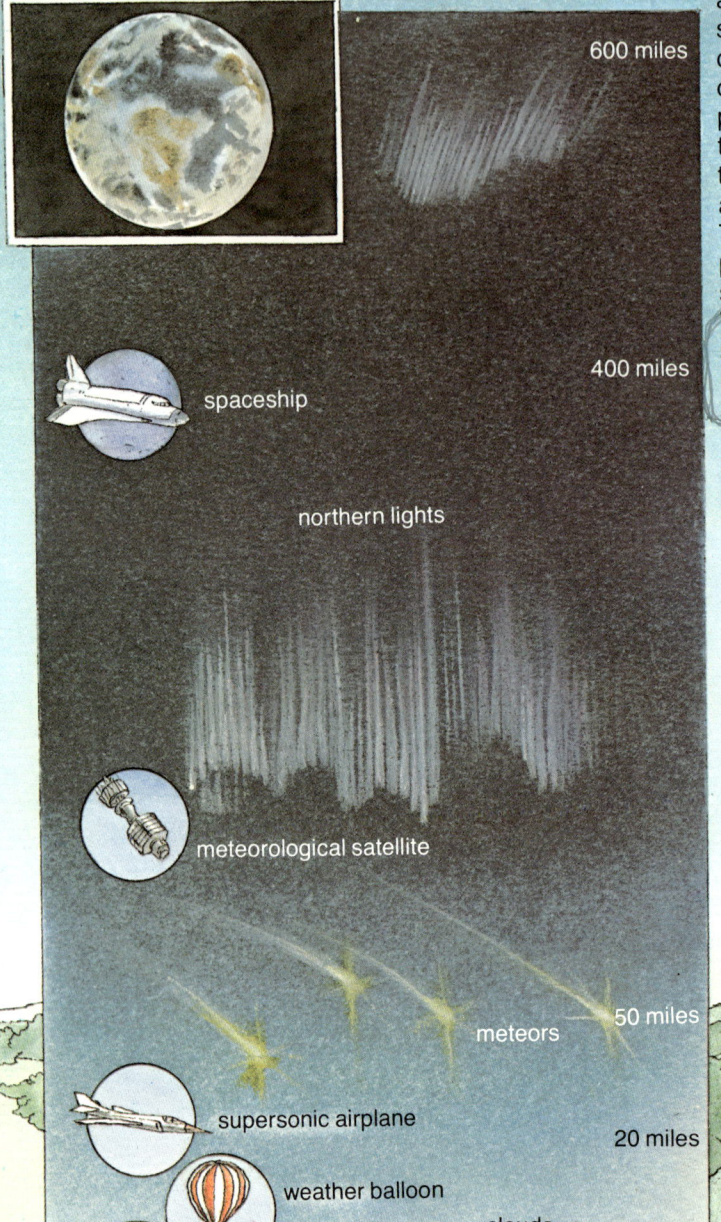

26

Storms occur when cold, dry air masses collide with warm, damp air masses. Cold dry air is much heavier than warm, damp air. It flows under warm air masses, causing high winds. At the same time it cools the water vapor so that droplets form and heavy rains or snows fall.

The barometer is one of the most important weather instruments. It measures air pressures. When the pressure drops rapidly a storm is on its way.

Why does it rain? When the sun shines on lakes and seas, water evaporates, just as it will from wet clothes. This means water vapor rises from the surface and goes into the air. When the vapor cools it turns into liquid water again. Tiny drops form clouds; bigger drops fall as rain.

Near an airport you often see a wind sock. It shows the direction of the wind, and in a general way, its speed. When no wind is blowing, the sock hangs down. A breeze will just lift it. A wind will fill it, as shown.

Weather balloons carry instruments high up into the atmosphere. Radio signals from the balloons send information to meteorologists on the ground. Such information helps them predict the weather.

tornado

People in cities receive hourly weather reports on the radio. Each day newspapers publish reports along with weather maps and photographs taken from weather satellites. These reports save thousands of lives each year by warning people about dangerous floods and tornadoes.

27

Rivers and Seas

Oceans cover 70.92% of the total surface of the earth. Ours is the water planet. No other planet in the solar system has such oceans.

Huge currents, such as the Gulf Stream, circulate the waters in the sea. Such currents moderate the temperature of the world by mixing hot and cool waters. The largest current is the Antarctic circumpolar current. Like all currents, it mixes oxygen and minerals in the water, and sea mammals and fish benefit.

Currents form because cold water is much heavier than warm water. As cold water sinks, it pulls warm water on the surface toward the region. Once this flow starts, it continues. Often winds also help push currents along.

To save fuel, ships often move along with sea currents.

The highest tides occur when the sun and moon line up as shown. Their gravity pulls the waters of the sea. These very high tides are called spring tides. When the moon and sun do not pull together, the high tides are not so high and are called neap tides. High tides occur about twice every 24 hours.

Waves, caused by winds or shifting tides, shape the shoreline. They cut sea cliffs, carry sand from beaches and make new beaches with it someplace else. They also mix oxygen and carbon dioxide into the water, which helps plants and animals.

The sea constantly rolls about and breaks up boulders, stones and sea shells until they finally become small particles. They make up the grains of sand covering the beaches.

Why does the sea change color? It reflects the color of the sky. If the sky is gray the sea will be gray, if blue it will be blue. Sometimes small one-celled plants and animals will color it reddish or make it greener.

Many volcanoes erupt at the bottom of the sea. On reaching the surface, volcanoes form islands, such as Iceland and the Hawaiian Islands. New islands, such as Surtsey, also form.

If the seas were drained of water, we would see a remarkable landscape of huge plains, volcanic peaks, great cliffs. Most impressive would be the Mid-Atlantic Ridge, which is a long underwater mountain range in the middle of the Atlantic Ocean.

How deep is the ocean? Away from the continents it averages 11,660 feet deep. Near the coasts it forms continental shelves which are part of the land masses and are only a few hundred feet deep.

Plankton is a mixture of tiny plants and animals, most of which are one-celled living beings. It floats on the surface of the oceans. In places there are vast areas of it. It is the main food source for all the other animals in the ocean. Often small animals such as little shrimp eat it, but so do some whales. Bigger fish eat the little fish and bigger ones eat them and so on. This is called a food chain.

At the bottom of the ocean live some strange fish as shown. They live in a world of utter darkness. They feed on dead plants and animals that drop downward in the water.

Rivers start flowing in several ways. Some start at melting glaciers. Most start as springs where rain waters, slowly creeping underground, come to the surface. Small brooks and streams eventually join with rivers, which flow to the ocean.

Many lakes lie in basins gouged out by glaciers.

Caves are hollowed out by slightly acid water which works its way into the ground, down cracks in limestone. The water is acid because carbon dioxide in the air mixes with it, forming carbonic acid. Over millions of years, this acid can eat out rooms to form large caves.

Many caves have streams and lakes in them. Sometimes rivers come gushing out as large springs. At other times the water seeps underground, where it can be reached by drills and pumped to the surface.

29

Ships and Their Ports

Most of the largest cities of the world are located next to the ocean or on rivers. Why is that? Rivers and oceans provide humans with their best and least expensive form of transportation. Not only that, but rivers that go to the ocean, and the oceans themselves, serve as waterways to the most distant lands and cities of the world.

Canals link up with other waterways. Dams on rivers provide electrical power. Seaweed can be gathered on the shores for fertilizer. Ocean beaches are popular with those seeking recreation.

Many sailors live most of their lives at sea. Families who live on barges usually have no other home aside from their barge.

The rivers and especially the seas provide millions of people with food, mainly fish. Many ships go to sea in search of fish. They may travel thousands of miles from their home port. Trawlers drag huge bag-shaped nets along the bottom of the ocean. The nets with the fish are hauled aboard. After being cleaned, the fish are frozen in refrigerators and carried back to a city to be sold.

Sonar is a device for sending out and receiving sound waves which go through the water. When the sound waves hit schools of fish, fishermen on the ship can tell where they are. Many modern devices help fishermen with their hard work.

At the same time scientists are trying to understand the life in the sea, so that fish will always be available for a hungry world.

Out on the open ocean far from land, sailors guide themselves with compasses. They indicate the directions: north, south, east, and west.

Since the sun sets in the west, the boy knows that if west is to his left, north must be straight ahead.

Humans think up many ways of using the seas and their huge resources. Different types of undersea craft have been made for exploring the depths of the ocean. Some do valuable work, such as work on deepwater oil rigs, or lifting things from sunken ships.

Whales are disappearing because of overhunting. We are also learning more about their intelligence. For these reasons, most countries now outlaw whale hunting, with or without harpoon cannons, such as the one shown.

Square traps are placed in bays to catch fish and shellfish. Buoys hold up nets, which will catch others.

At this sea farm, people are raising fish and shellfish, such as oysters, as farmers on land would raise cattle or chickens. Sea farms produce more and more food each year.

Large salt basins are filled with sea water. The heat of the sun evaporates the water and leaves salt behind, gathered in piles as shown.

In the near future, ships may tow huge icebergs to cities which lack enough fresh water for drinking. The icebergs will melt, supplying drinkable water.

deep sea submarines

sonar

robot explorer submarine

nodule

Divers using scuba equipment explore shallow areas of the sea. Special submarines go deeper, and bathyscaphes have gone to the very deepest part of the ocean, the Marianas Trench, 35,820 feet deep.

Every year humans learn more about the seas, which are the last frontier on earth. Strange and wonderful plants and animals are found, some of which are unlike any others ever known before. Discoveries of wrecked ships and ruined cities, now lying under the waves, have helped us to understand our own history better.

Many valuable resources lie at the bottom of the oceans. Not only are oil and gas being recovered, but there are mineral ores as well.

Some are in the form of nodules which contain manganese, nickel, cobalt, and iron, all of which are useful.

Hundreds of millions of dollars worth of gold is known to be in shipwrecks lying on the ocean floor, along with many other man-made valuables: silver plates, steel ships, and so on.

31

Hot and Cold

Why do we have summer and winter? During our summer in the Northern Hemisphere, the earth is tilted on its axis toward the sun, so it is warmer. In winter, the earth tilts away from the sun, so it is colder.

Mammals and birds have fur or feathers to protect them from the cold.

Turtles, snakes, fish, lizards and frogs are cold-blooded, which means the temperature of their blood is the same as the air around them.

Mammals and birds are warm-blooded, which means that their bodies stay at the same temperature all the time. Humans have a normal body temperature of 98.6°F (37°C). We stay at this temperature whether the air around us is hot or cold. When we have a higher temperature we have a fever.

Because we lack fur and perspire easily, we are less protected from the cold than other mammals. But we have invented many ways of keeping warm with clothes, fireplaces, and central heating in our homes. Sometimes, though, we are too warm; so fans, parasols, and air conditioners were invented. These solutions to weather problems enable humans to live in more places on earth than any other animal.

One of man's most important inventions was the making of fire. Before then, he probably got fire from burning trees, hit by lightning. Thanks to fire, we can eat many foods, such as beans, rice, bread, etc., that must be cooked. Fires also warm us. Energy for power comes from fire and heat. Metals can be heated until they melt and can be molded into different shapes.

By boiling milk, fruits and vegetables, we kill the germs and microbes that would make them spoil. Canning these foods while they are boiling hot, lets them keep for months. Icy cold does not kill germs, but it can stop them from developing. That is why frozen foods can last for long periods of time.

thermos bottle

liquid
outer cover
vacuum

Insulation stops the flow of heat from one place to another. A sparrow's feathers, for example, insulate the bird, stopping its body heat from flowing away into the air. Down and woolen clothing insulate us. Double brick walls and double glass windows help insulate a house, for trapped air is a good insulator. Refrigerators are insulated with fiber glass or polystyrene.

To keep liquids hot for hours, we use thermos bottles. Inside them is a vacuum, which is an empty space that has no air or anything else in it. It is difficult for heat to pass through a vacuum, so things inside the thermos stay hot as the heat will not escape.

Part Two: Inside the Human Body

Digestion and Circulation

What do we need every day in order to have healthy bodies? Oxygen, which is in the air, and water. Our bodies contain 60% to 70% water.

We need food: proteins — found in meat, fish, eggs, milk and cheese.

Fats and oils — in butter, olive oil, and other substances.

Sugars and starches — in sugar, honey, rice, pasta, bread, potatoes.

Calories measure the amount of energy we get from foods. From ages 6 to 10 we need 1,600 calories per day; everyone else needs 1,800 to 4,000 per day.

We also need vitamins — found in raw fruits, vegetables, milk, grains, and eggs; minerals — salt, iron and phosphorus — found in many vegetables and fish; calcium — in milk; cellulose, as fiber to help digestion — found in grains, fruits and vegetables.

In spite of eating food, we would starve if it were not digested. So food is broken down and dissolved chemically in the stomach and is carried by the blood to every cell. The digestive system is composed of the long alimentary canal or tube together with digestive glands and chemicals.

The job of the respiratory system is to get oxygen in the air to the blood which carries it to each cell. The system is composed of lungs, blood vessels, and heart which pumps the blood.

How do we digest our food?

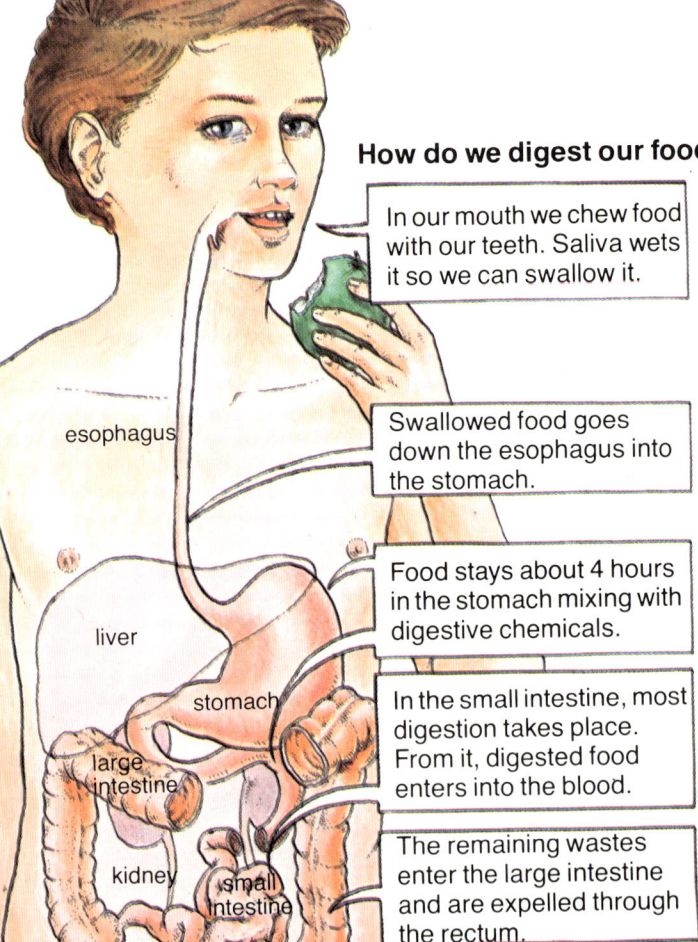

In our mouth we chew food with our teeth. Saliva wets it so we can swallow it.

Swallowed food goes down the esophagus into the stomach.

Food stays about 4 hours in the stomach mixing with digestive chemicals.

In the small intestine, most digestion takes place. From it, digested food enters into the blood.

The remaining wastes enter the large intestine and are expelled through the rectum.

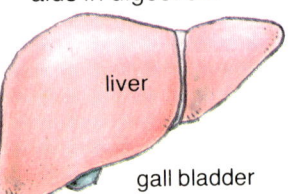

The liver filters the blood. If we eat too many sugars or fats, it stores part of them. It produces a liquid, bile, which aids in digestion.

Kidneys remove extra water and urea from the blood. Urea results from the breakdown of protein foods. The water and urea expelled from the kidneys is urine, which flows to the bladder.

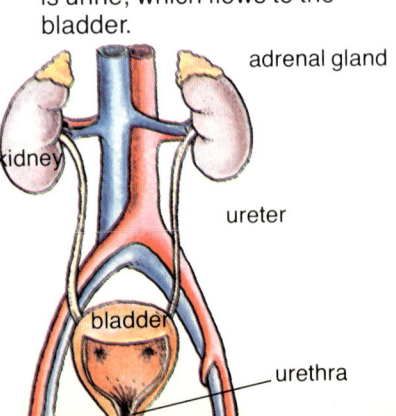

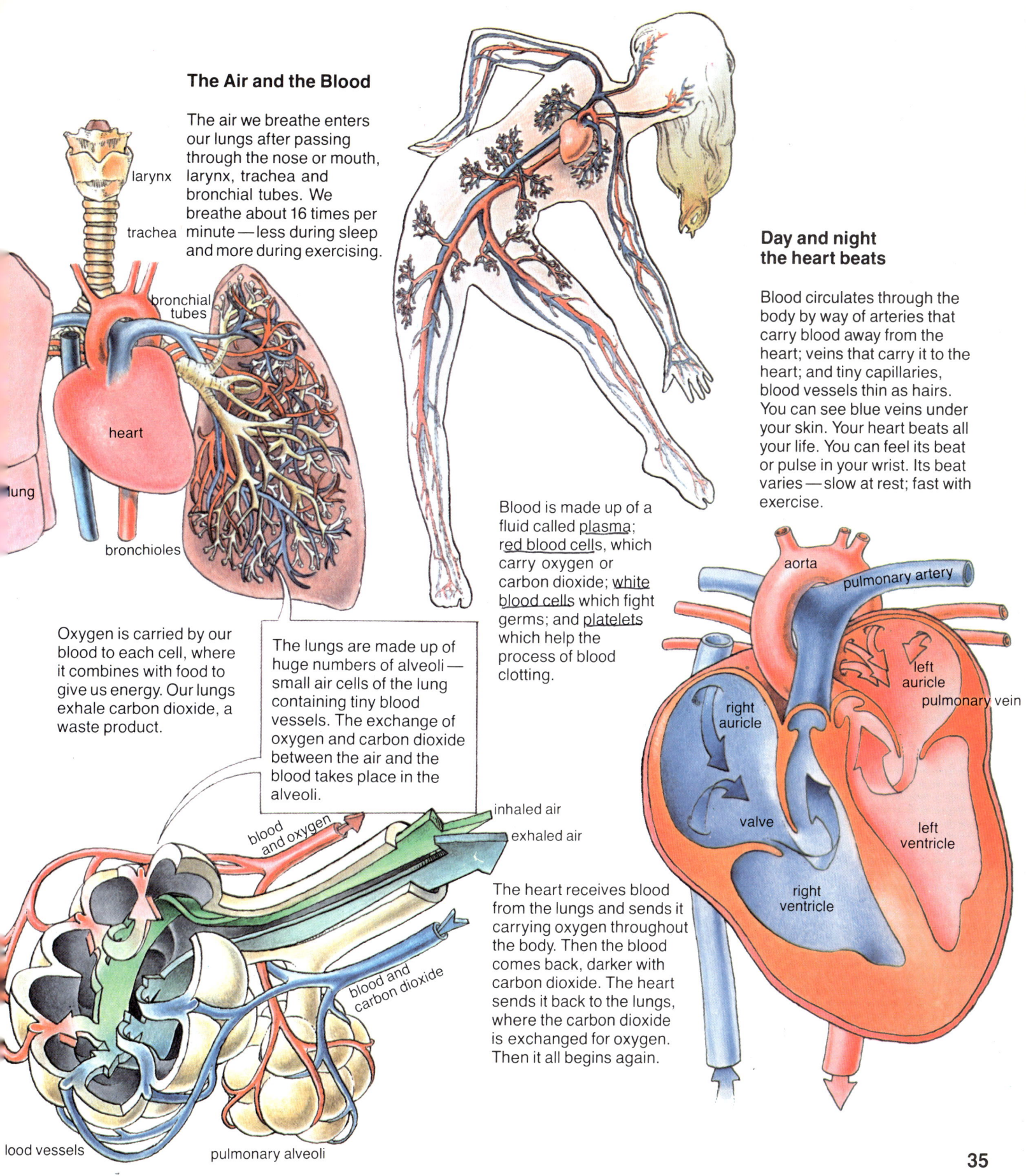

The Skeleton and Muscles

**Our skeleton supports us.
Our muscles move us.**

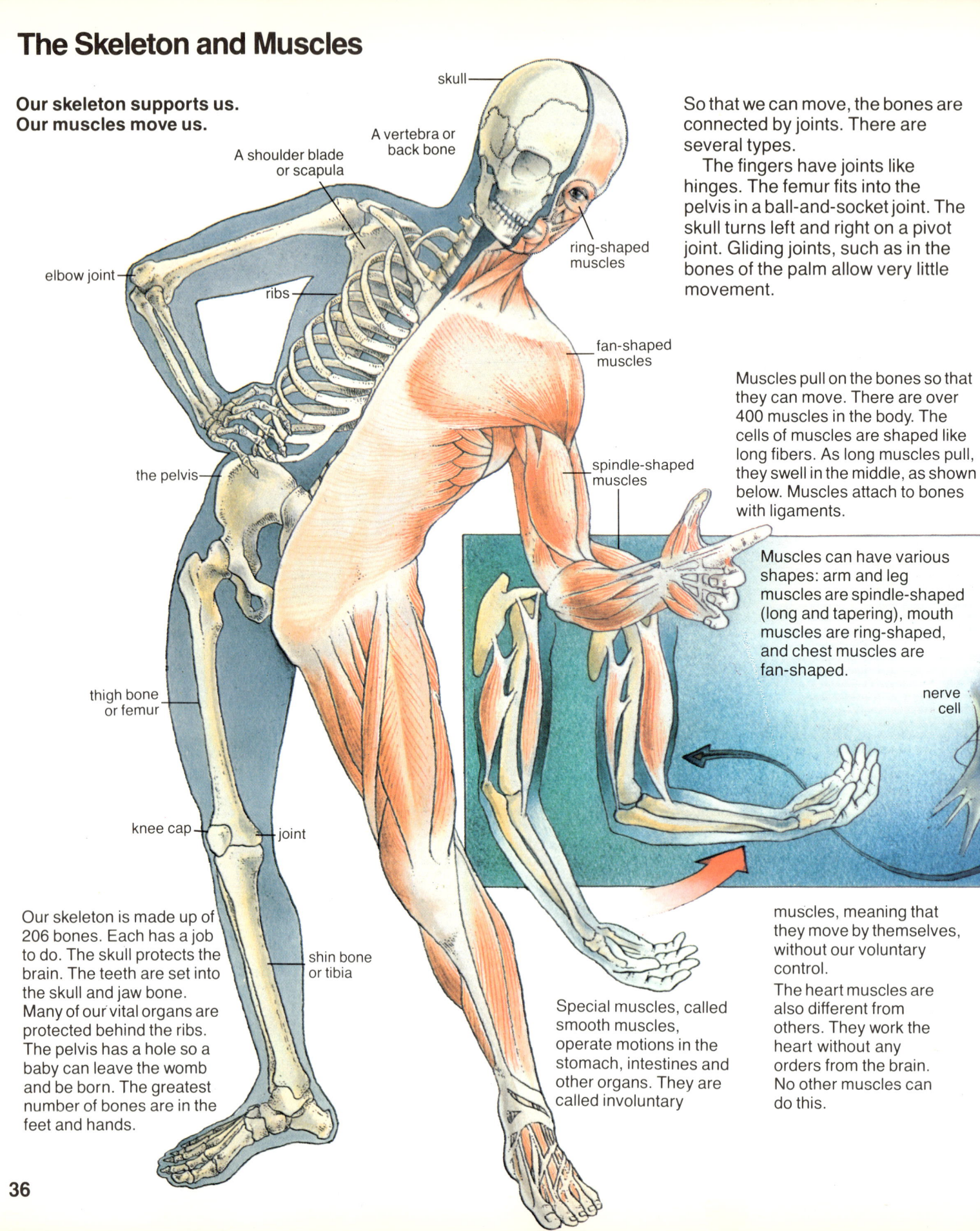

So that we can move, the bones are connected by joints. There are several types.

The fingers have joints like hinges. The femur fits into the pelvis in a ball-and-socket joint. The skull turns left and right on a pivot joint. Gliding joints, such as in the bones of the palm allow very little movement.

Muscles pull on the bones so that they can move. There are over 400 muscles in the body. The cells of muscles are shaped like long fibers. As long muscles pull, they swell in the middle, as shown below. Muscles attach to bones with ligaments.

Muscles can have various shapes: arm and leg muscles are spindle-shaped (long and tapering), mouth muscles are ring-shaped, and chest muscles are fan-shaped.

Our skeleton is made up of 206 bones. Each has a job to do. The skull protects the brain. The teeth are set into the skull and jaw bone. Many of our vital organs are protected behind the ribs. The pelvis has a hole so a baby can leave the womb and be born. The greatest number of bones are in the feet and hands.

Special muscles, called smooth muscles, operate motions in the stomach, intestines and other organs. They are called involuntary muscles, meaning that they move by themselves, without our voluntary control.

The heart muscles are also different from others. They work the heart without any orders from the brain. No other muscles can do this.

36

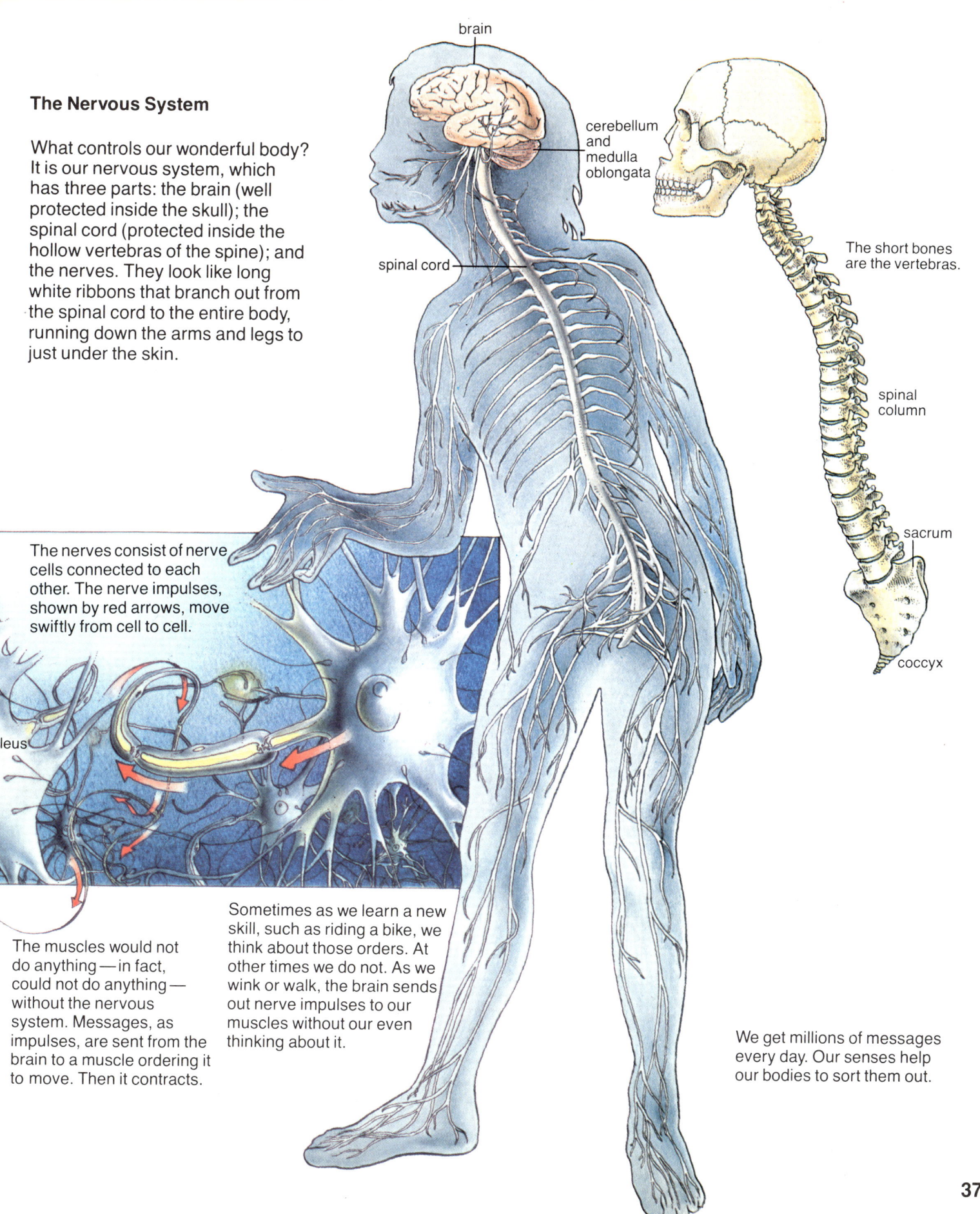

The Nervous System

What controls our wonderful body? It is our nervous system, which has three parts: the brain (well protected inside the skull); the spinal cord (protected inside the hollow vertebras of the spine); and the nerves. They look like long white ribbons that branch out from the spinal cord to the entire body, running down the arms and legs to just under the skin.

The nerves consist of nerve cells connected to each other. The nerve impulses, shown by red arrows, move swiftly from cell to cell.

The muscles would not do anything — in fact, could not do anything — without the nervous system. Messages, as impulses, are sent from the brain to a muscle ordering it to move. Then it contracts.

Sometimes as we learn a new skill, such as riding a bike, we think about those orders. At other times we do not. As we wink or walk, the brain sends out nerve impulses to our muscles without our even thinking about it.

The short bones are the vertebras.

We get millions of messages every day. Our senses help our bodies to sort them out.

Our Senses

We understand the world we live in because of our sense organs: our eyes, ears, noses; taste buds in our tongues; organs that detect pain, especially in our skin; and organs which give us a sense of balance.

Messages from these organs go to the brain, which interprets and deciphers them. The messages travel through the nervous system, much in the way that electricity flows in wires. Some important messages, especially of pain, trigger reflexes. In this case, the messages do not go all the way to the brain. They go to nerves in the spinal column, which cause reflex actions. An example of a reflex action is shown when we automatically jerk our hand away from a hot stove.

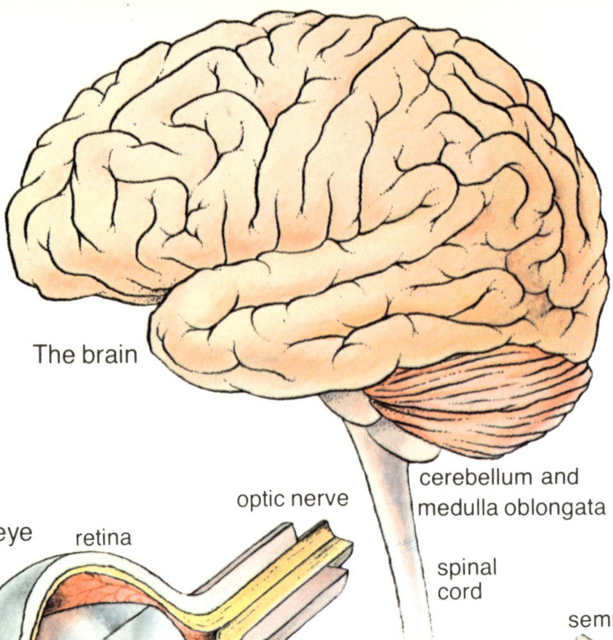

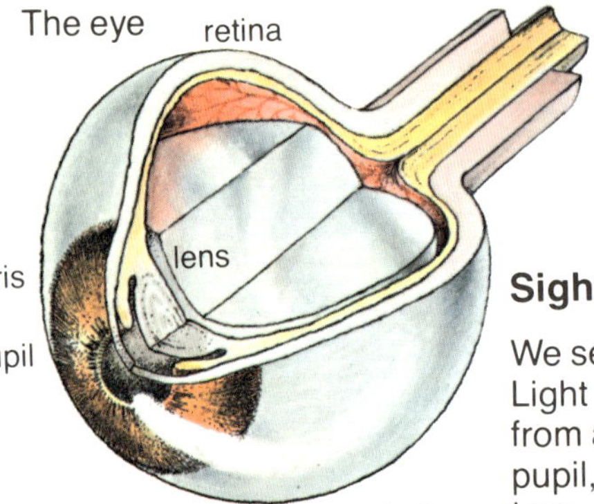

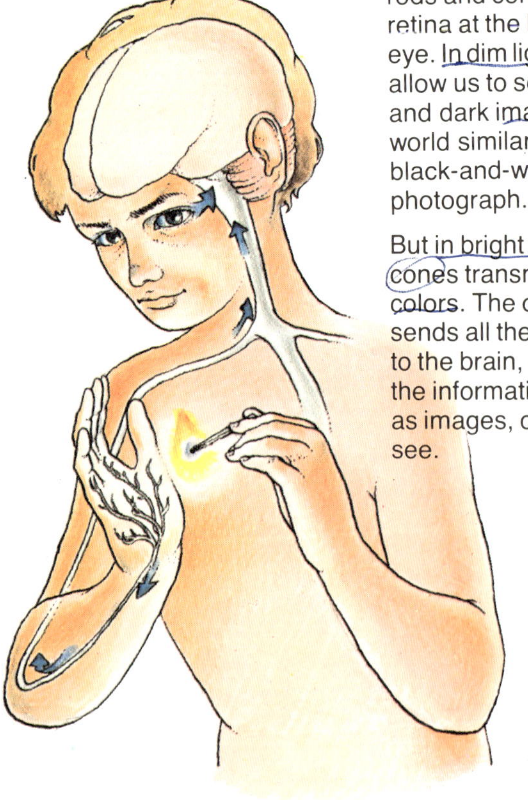

How does this boy know about the flaming match which could burn him? First of all, he can feel the flame's heat because of special nerve endings in the skin which detect heat and cold. They send messages to the brain. At the same time, the boy can see the flaming match. Optic nerves in the eye send their messages to the brain. Once the brain deciphers the messages, the boy can decide what to do. He can blow it out, use it to light a candle, and so on.

The brain

cerebellum and medulla oblongata

optic nerve

spinal cord

The eye — retina, iris, pupil, lens, eyeball

Sight

We see with our eyes. Light sent or reflected from an object enters the pupil, passes through the lens, and stimulates the rods and cones in the retina at the back of the eye. In dim light, the rods allow us to see light and dark images, or a world similar to a black-and-white photograph.

But in bright light the cones transmit mainly colors. The optic nerve sends all the messages to the brain, which puts the information together as images, or what we see.

Hearing

We hear with organs in our ears. Sounds make waves in the air, somewhat like ripples in water made from a dropped stone. Waves strike the eardrum, which transmits them to tiny bones of the middle ear: the hammer, anvil and stirrup. They magnify the power of the waves 22 times and send them into the cochlea, which is filled with fluid and tiny hairs. These are attached to nerve endings which send messages to the brain.

semicircular canals, hammer, anvil, outer ear, cochlea, stirrup, ear canal, eardrum

The ear

38

The Sense of Balance

How can we tell if we are right side up or upside down? How do we feel a sense of balance? Near the cochlea are three semicircular canals. Each contains fluid which acts something like a level. If we move, the liquid moves, washing against hairs attached to nerve endings, which send messages to our brain. It sends out messages to our muscles which move so we stay upright or balanced.

The Skin and Sense of Touch

Nerve endings in the skin respond to cold, heat, pain, pleasure, and can also tell if objects are smooth or rough.

Our skin protects us. It keeps the body underneath from drying out. It also keeps out most germs. Sweat glands help control our body temperature if we are too hot. Blood vessels in the skin become smaller, allowing less heat loss if we are cold. Both our hair and nails grow from the skin.

Taste

On our tongues are taste buds. With them we can tell if something tastes sweet, salty, sour, or bitter. For other tastes we need to smell things as well.

Where Does the Voice Come From?

Vocal cords vibrate when we speak and force air through them. We control an opening in them, making it larger or smaller. This changes sounds coming through them. To pronounce words, we use our tongue, teeth and lips. Look in a mirror and say —A, E, I, O, U, B, D, L, M. Surprised?

Smell

Odors move with the air. They enter our nostrils and stimulate the olfactory cells, located inside the nose. Odors affect the taste of food. If our nose is stuffed up from a cold, foods lose much of their taste.

39

Our Bodies' Defenses

Our bodies defend themselves all the time from diseases. They also heal themselves.

Diseases are caused by microbes: <u>protozoans</u>, which are one-celled animals, such as malaria; <u>bacteria</u>, one-celled plants, such as the one which causes typhoid fever; and <u>viruses</u>, which are very tiny particles resembling both living and nonliving material. They cause diseases, such as influenza. Our blood plasma has antibodies in it—special chemicals that can fight and destroy microbes. The white cells of the blood can attack and eat microbes.

Our bodies can repair damage done to them. Broken bones, for example, can grow together and heal.

If we eat too much or happen to eat or drink a poison, we will vomit it up to get rid of it.

If we get too cold, we will shiver. This action will heat us up again, for it is a strenuous exercise.

If we begin to dry out, messages will be sent to our brain which we interpret as thirst.

We do not stop breathing in our sleep, for carbon dioxide would build up in our blood stream. This too will trigger messages which go to the brain. Even as we sleep, the brain will make us breathe again.

Our bodies are wonderfully designed to protect, defend and help us.

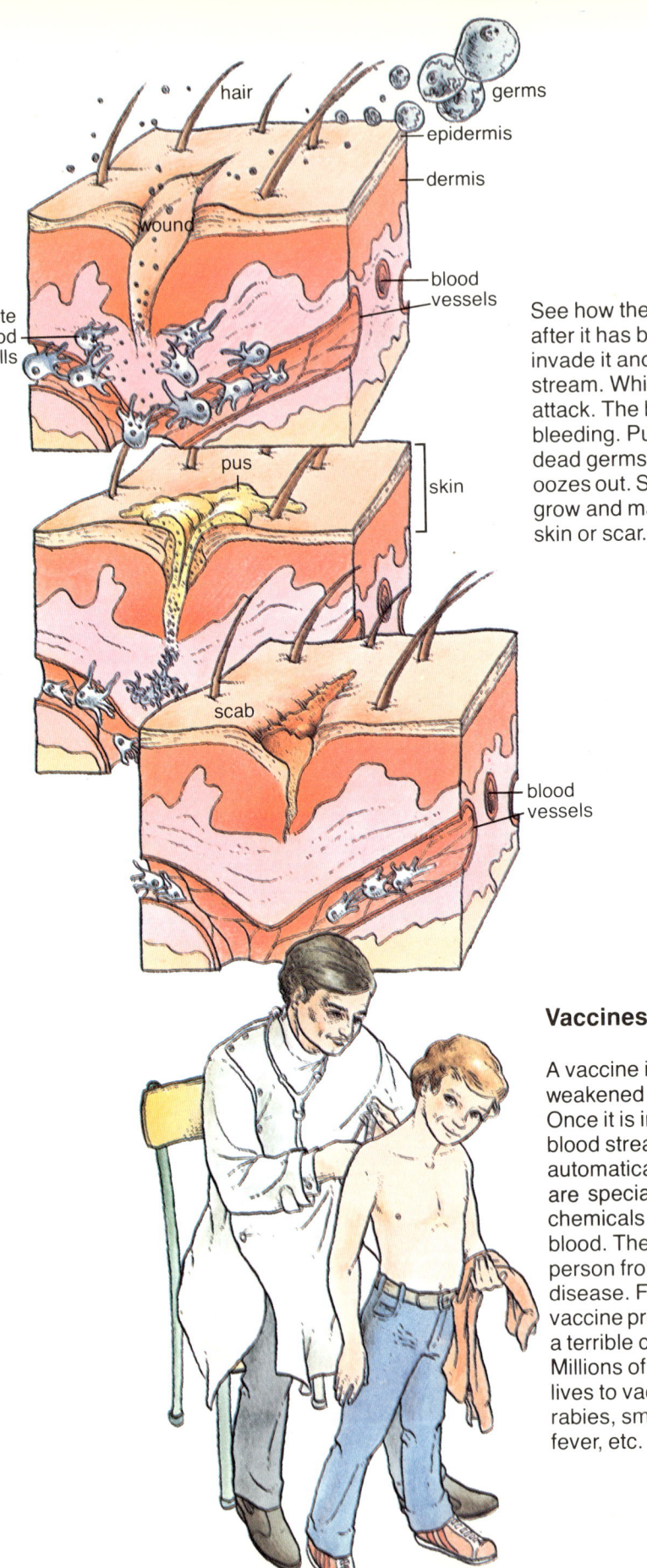

See how the skin heals itself after it has been cut. Germs invade it and reach the blood stream. White blood cells attack. The blood clots to stop bleeding. Pus, consisting of dead germs and white cells, oozes out. Soon new skin cells grow and make a new patch of skin or scar.

Vaccines

A vaccine is a preparation of weakened or killed germs. Once it is injected into the blood stream, antibodies form automatically. Antibodies are special germ-fighting chemicals produced by the blood. They will protect a person from a specific disease. For example, a polio vaccine protects us from polio, a terrible crippling disease. Millions of people owe their lives to vaccines against rabies, smallpox, typhoid fever, etc.

The Glands

Glands produce important substances needed by our bodies. Some produce familiar fluids — saliva, sweat and tears. Others produce hormones, chemicals essential for health and growth. Hormones are released directly into the bloodstream and into the lymph, a colorless fluid that surrounds the cells.

To keep our bodies healthy and in good shape, we should exercise, bathe, and be well groomed.

tear glands
salivary glands
sweat glands
mammary glands
pituitary gland
thyroid glands
adrenal glands
pancreas
ovary

Brushing the teeth twice a day gets rid of food wastes that would become breeding grounds for germs in our mouths, causing cavities.

enamel
ivory
dentin
pulp
gum
jaw bone
blood vessels
tooth nerve

We have 32 teeth, each with a different job to do. The 8 front teeth, the incisors, cut food. The 4 sharp canines grip food. The 20 molars grind food. Babies have 20 teeth, called milk teeth, which they lose at about age six. Each tooth has enamel on the outside. It is white and very hard, but can get cavities. Under it is dentin which is like bone. In the center is pulp made up of blood vessels and the tooth nerve. The tooth is anchored in the jaw bone. The gum helps to hold it in place.

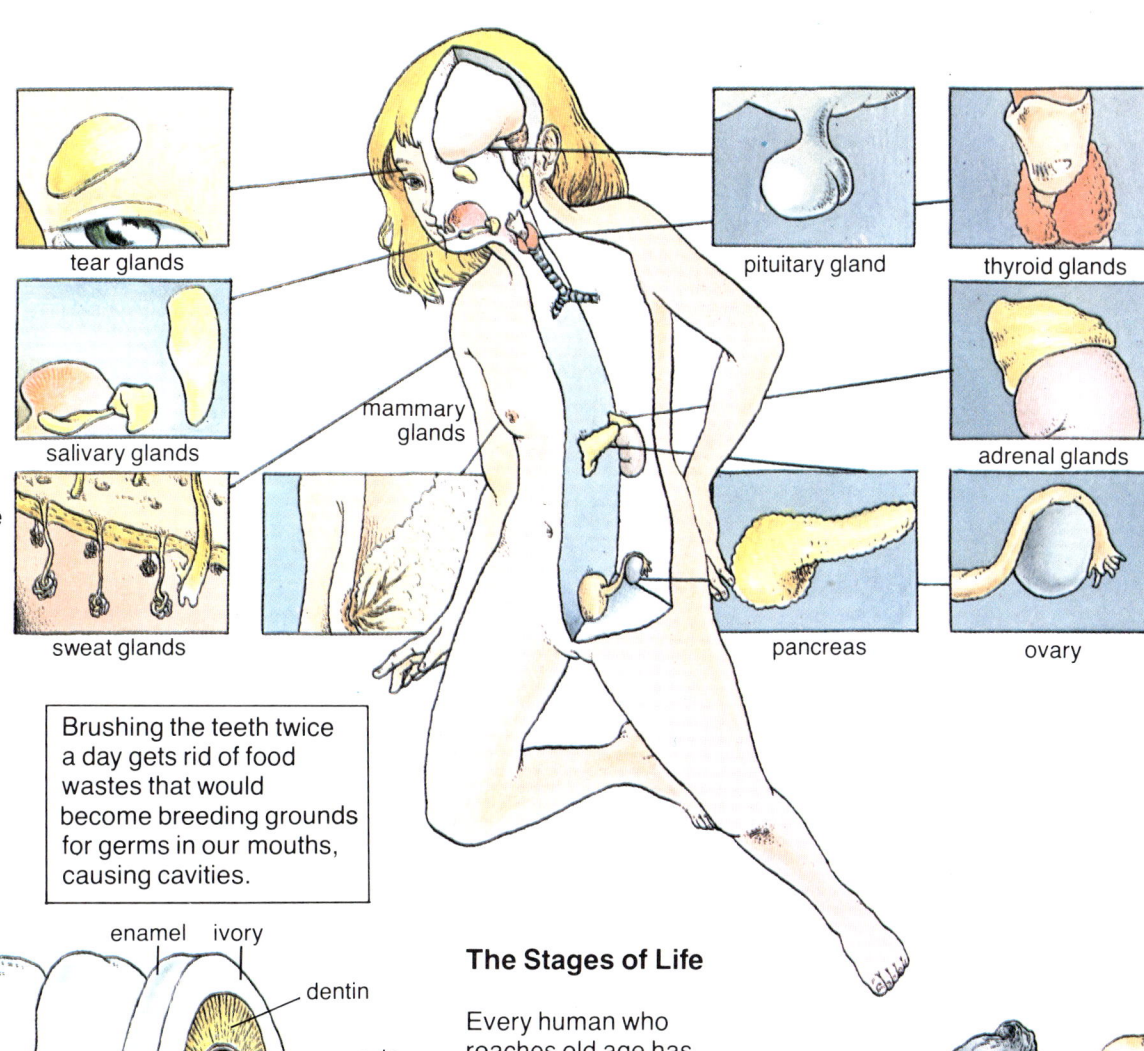

The Stages of Life

Every human who reaches old age has gone through the various stages of life. From the time we are born our bodies change. Many of the changes have to do with hormones, which influence the way our bodies grow and operate. Girls grow taller until about age 14 and boys to age 18. In old age, hormone production slows down. The skin wrinkles, the hair becomes gray and a person tires more easily. Many old people enjoy life, especially when they can be with young people, who enjoy their discussions of other places and other times.

Reproduction

All living beings, plants and animals, can reproduce themselves. That is, they can bring forth offspring or young which resemble themselves. For example, oak trees reproduce new oaks, dogs have puppies, and humans have babies.

A human being starts life when a male spermatozoan enters a female ovum. That moment is called conception. The ovum, which is a single cell, divides in two, four, eight, and so on until a fetus is developed. A fetus is a baby which has not yet been born.

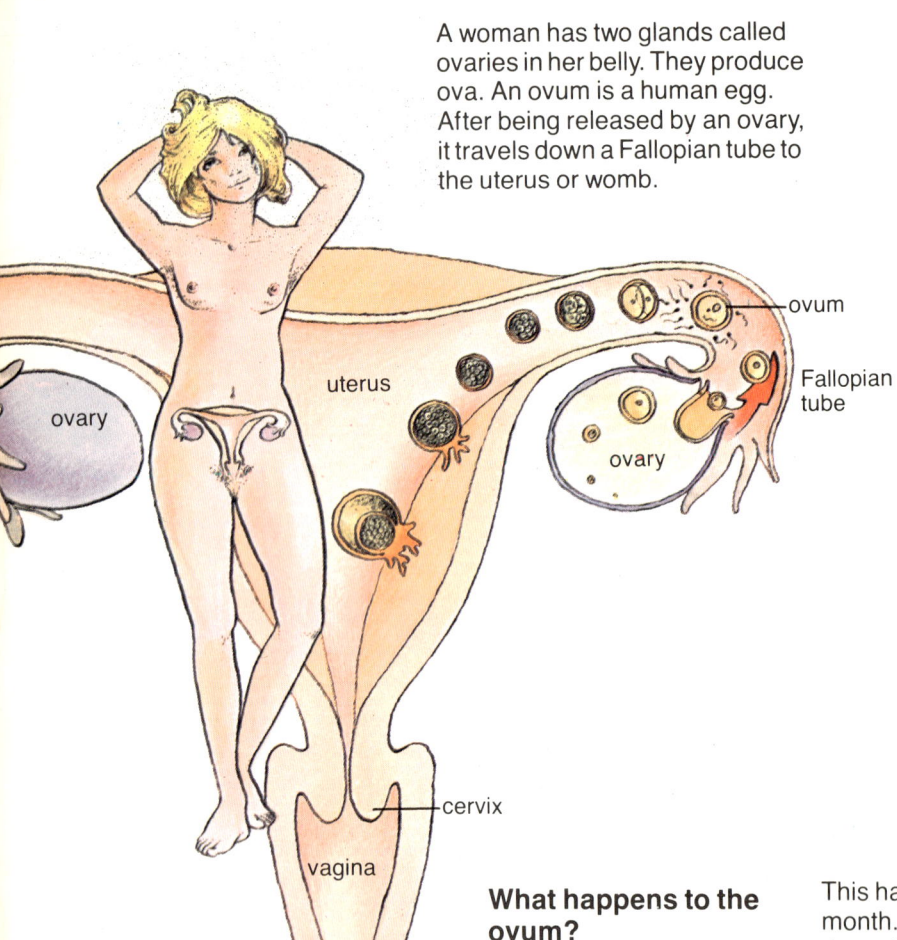

A woman has two glands called ovaries in her belly. They produce ova. An ovum is a human egg. After being released by an ovary, it travels down a Fallopian tube to the uterus or womb.

A man has two special glands, testicles, which constantly produce billions of spermatozoans or sperm. They are discharged through the penis.

What happens to the ovum?

If the ovum is not fertilized by a spermatozoan, the mucous lining of the uterus is discharged with a small amount of blood. The woman menstruates. This happens once a month. If a spermatozoan, deposited by a man's penis in the vagina, fertilizes the ovum, conception takes place and menstruation ceases until after the birth of the baby.

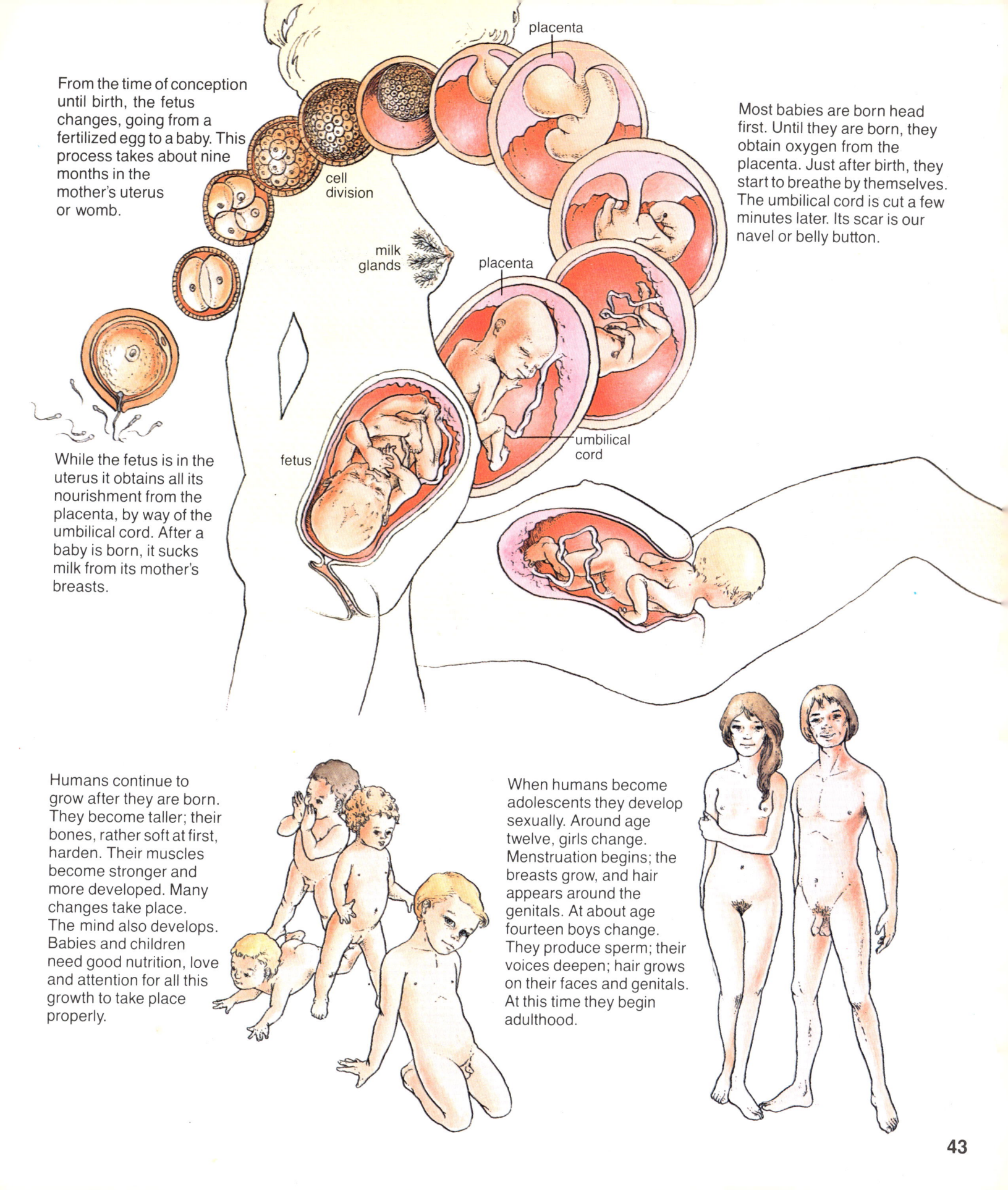

From the time of conception until birth, the fetus changes, going from a fertilized egg to a baby. This process takes about nine months in the mother's uterus or womb.

cell division

milk glands

placenta

placenta

fetus

umbilical cord

Most babies are born head first. Until they are born, they obtain oxygen from the placenta. Just after birth, they start to breathe by themselves. The umbilical cord is cut a few minutes later. Its scar is our navel or belly button.

While the fetus is in the uterus it obtains all its nourishment from the placenta, by way of the umbilical cord. After a baby is born, it sucks milk from its mother's breasts.

Humans continue to grow after they are born. They become taller; their bones, rather soft at first, harden. Their muscles become stronger and more developed. Many changes take place. The mind also develops. Babies and children need good nutrition, love and attention for all this growth to take place properly.

When humans become adolescents they develop sexually. Around age twelve, girls change. Menstruation begins; the breasts grow, and hair appears around the genitals. At about age fourteen boys change. They produce sperm; their voices deepen; hair grows on their faces and genitals. At this time they begin adulthood.

43

Part Three: People and Society

Life in the Past

The earth is about 4.6 billion years old. Much of its past is unknown to us. However, we do find fossils, bones, skeletons, and even the furry hides of mammoths. (See picture.) They tell us a great deal about life in the past. We also find prehistoric human remains, such as skeletons, cave paintings, stone spear tips, human hand prints, and most important of all, skulls. Because of such finds, we can reconstruct some of the daily life of our ancestors. See the picture for such a reconstruction.

What have such finds shown us about the past? First, they show us that plant and animal species of millions of years ago were different from those of today. This snail-like creature (see picture) is an ammonite. Ammonites died out millions of years ago; that is, they became extinct.

Some species died out, while others changed slowly over time. Modern elephants, for example, are the relatives of prehistoric mammoths which became extinct. Many generations were necessary to transform one species into another. Such a change is called evolution.

Interestingly, we can tell from old fossils and bones that humans have evolved from earlier primates. Primates are animals like monkeys, apes and humans, which have thumbs and eyes that look toward the front. About 3 million years ago some primates, which were not apes, began to look like humans. They walked upright. Their bodies and skulls were smaller than ours. Compared to the rest of the skull, they had large jaws. Several species evolved, each one taller than the last, with larger skulls, bigger brains and smaller jaws.

Finally, about 35,000 years ago our own species, Homo sapiens sapiens, appeared on earth. Homo sapiens sapiens developed better hunting tools, painted cave pictures, and traveled all over the world, inhabiting almost all of it.

About 4,000 B.C. humans developed civilizations, which means they grew crops, built cities and had some form of writing. The remains of ancient Egypt, Mexico, Greece, China and Rome tell us much about how people lived in those times.

ammonite

mammoth

The human skull has changed over the last million years. On the far left is an Australopithecus skull, 1 million years old; the middle is a Sinanthropus skull 500,000 years old. At the right is a modern Homo sapiens sapiens.

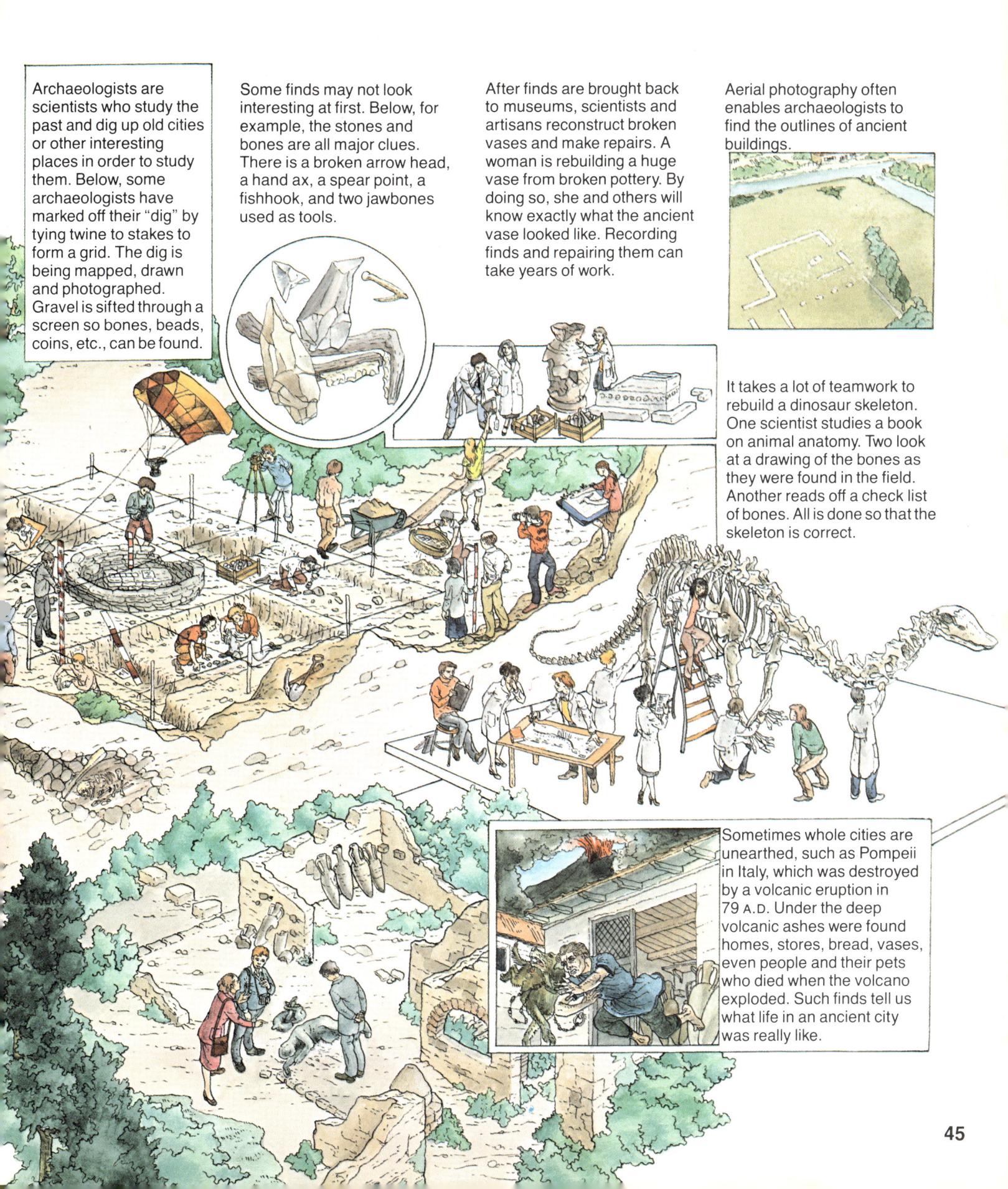

Archaeologists are scientists who study the past and dig up old cities or other interesting places in order to study them. Below, some archaeologists have marked off their "dig" by tying twine to stakes to form a grid. The dig is being mapped, drawn and photographed. Gravel is sifted through a screen so bones, beads, coins, etc., can be found.

Some finds may not look interesting at first. Below, for example, the stones and bones are all major clues. There is a broken arrow head, a hand ax, a spear point, a fishhook, and two jawbones used as tools.

After finds are brought back to museums, scientists and artisans reconstruct broken vases and make repairs. A woman is rebuilding a huge vase from broken pottery. By doing so, she and others will know exactly what the ancient vase looked like. Recording finds and repairing them can take years of work.

Aerial photography often enables archaeologists to find the outlines of ancient buildings.

It takes a lot of teamwork to rebuild a dinosaur skeleton. One scientist studies a book on animal anatomy. Two look at a drawing of the bones as they were found in the field. Another reads off a check list of bones. All is done so that the skeleton is correct.

Sometimes whole cities are unearthed, such as Pompeii in Italy, which was destroyed by a volcanic eruption in 79 A.D. Under the deep volcanic ashes were found homes, stores, bread, vases, even people and their pets who died when the volcano exploded. Such finds tell us what life in an ancient city was really like.

45

Shelters

All humans need shelter for warmth, protection, and as a place to store weapons and tools, to sleep, cook, and so on.

Some, but not all, early humans lived in caves.

Native Americans invented the teepee, a home that could be easily put up and taken down and transported from place to place.

In the tropics, people built large huts thatched with dome-shaped roofs.

Lake dwellers of Europe built their homes over water as a protection against enemies and wild animals. The houses rested on stakes driven into the muddy lake bottoms.

The American pioneers built log cabins. There was plenty of timber. All they needed was an ax.

In Europe some people built houses of stones. In Africa, Asia, and North America, people lived in dwellings of sun-dried brick or adobe.

Some shelters were placed with safety in mind. A cave high above a cliff could protect the people inside; so could a house in the middle of a lake.

Bricks are made of baked clay in factories.

Nomads are people who are almost always on the move with herds of animals. They live in tents that are easily put up and taken down.

Whenever they move, the tents are carried by their camels. Many campers today use tents, for they are so convenient and easy to take from place to place.

Many people live on boats or river barges. Pictured also is a Chinese houseboat or junk.

Gypsies live in modern trailers or, sometimes, in their colorful old-fashioned wagons. All the time they travel from place to place with their belongings.

Large numbers of the world's people do not have enough money for a decent home. They live in old cars or shacks and lean-tos.

Most people in the world now live in cities. They live in apartments or high-rise buildings. These are built on a steel framework. Some are over twenty stories high. Many others live in houses built of cement blocks mortared together with cement. The cement is mixed with sand and water.

47

A Day in the City

Most people today live in cities, and most of the world's cities are very much the same. In Paris, New York, London, or Toronto people do the same activities.

Everyone fits into the complicated life of his or her city. Each person has a place to go and something to do.

Here, everyone is busy. A father walks his two girls to school. Passengers get on a bus and will ride it. The driver is probably on the third loop of his route for the morning. The man on crutches may be going to see his doctor. People are having packages weighed at a post office. A policeman has his hands full trying to keep the traffic moving.

Cooks are preparing meals in a restaurant. Street musicians receive some coins from a passerby. A man on a motor bike delivers a message. Office workers are starting their day. But one woman is late!

A man delivers papers to a newsstand, where people are eager to read the headlines and buy magazines. Shoppers choose fish, fruit, and vegetables at a market, while more produce is being delivered. A meter inspector gives someone a parking ticket. Two friends meet near a telephone booth, where someone phones. At a coffee shop the morning rush is about to begin. A customer signals for a waiter. Two delivery men bring beverages to the counter. Outside, workmen repair water pipes below the street. An ambulance speeds around a corner, taking a sick person to a hospital. In classrooms school teachers wait for pupils to arrive. In the supermarket, shoppers line up at the checkout counters, while cashiers ring up their purchases.

It takes thousands, even millions of people to run a large city every day, doesn't it? Does this city remind you of the place where you live?

49

Energy and How We Use It

We get energy from many sources: oil; natural gas; running water; the wind; nuclear power, and so on. We use this energy in engines so that they can do work for us. They lift, transport things, turn electric fans, move chain saws. Energy is defined as the capacity to do work.

Our civilization is built upon the use of huge quantities of energy. Without energy supplies and engines and machines, we would have no passenger ships, no skyscrapers, no huge dams, no airplanes. Without energy supplies and engines we would probably live as the ancient Romans did.

No wonder energy supplies are so important! This explains why people worry about energy shortages. But it also explains why geologists look for new supplies of coal and oil, and why scientists are trying to obtain energy from the sun, the atom, the wind, and so on.

The tall windmill with streamlined blades is a modern version of the old-fashioned windmill to its left. But it produces thousands of times more energy and provides electricity for homes.

Old-fashioned water wheels used to grind wheat into flour for people who lived in small towns. The fan-shaped wheel in the dam is a modern turbine which supplies electric power.

The energy in steam can easily lift the lid from a pot of boiling water. In the same way, steam can push a piston inside a cylinder. As the cylinder moves back and forth, the linked rods will turn the wheel. The steam engine is racing down the tracks.

Another steam engine is the steam turbine. It works like the water turbine in the dam above. Steam hitting fans in the engine turns them at very high speed. Steam turbines are the most powerful engines of all.

A gasoline engine also has pistons and cylinders. Gasoline and air in a cylinder explode. The force of the explosion pushes the piston. As it goes back and forth, it turns the wheel.

How do you get electricity in your home? First a supply of oil, natural gas, or coal is found. If it is oil or gas, workers drill in the ground to bring it to the surface. At a refinery, crude oil is made into fuel oil, kerosene and gasoline. A power plant burns the oil to heat steam which powers turbines and electrical generators (special machines for making electricity). High voltage lines carry the electricity over a long distance to your town. Coal, on the other hand, is mined and sent to power plants by freight trains.

We may use natural gas to heat our stoves. It is shipped to us by long underground pipes.

What is electricity? An electrical current is a current of electrons. As we saw on page 11, atoms have electrons. They can be stripped away from an atom and made to flow, and that is what electricity is.

oil refinery

coal mine

nuclear power plant

solar mirror

Scientists are trying more and more to use nuclear power. There are two ways of getting energy from atoms. A very large uranium atom can be split into smaller atoms, giving off energy; this is called fission. Or, two small hydrogen atoms can be forced to fuse together to make helium. When they do, energy is given off. That is called fusion. We already use fission energy, but scientists are still experimenting with fusion energy. Someday it may also be a source of energy for electrical power.

solar house

Scientists think that the sun will shine for another five billion years. No wonder people want to use its energy. We already do. Many houses are heated by solar energy, such as the house to the left. Huge mirrors have been built that can focus the sun's light and heat in one place, where it is hot enough to melt steel. Scientists are thinking of building mirrors in space to collect sunlight. Its heat will produce electricity that can be collected on earth.

Machines and Computers

Machines are part of our daily lives. We use them all the time—bicycles, egg beaters, television sets, and so on. We also enjoy making things with tools and machines, be they simply knitting needles, pieces of wood, paper and twine, or more complicated tools like wrenches for repairing bicycles. Or we may work in a huge factory where cars or computers are made. Humans are defined as the tool-making animals. This is true. We could not exist without tools and machines.

Many machines are made just so they can manufacture other machines. In an automobile factory dozens of machines help workers produce cars, which are also machines. Our civilization depends on huge factories for cars, television sets, and so on. The factories are very efficient because the work is broken down into many steps. Each worker does one job.

Calculators and computers are revolutionizing all our industries. They also help business people to keep records and students to do their homework. They are electronic devices that can do complicated calculations in a split second.

Computers are programmed: that is, they are given sets of instructions. They may be told when to add, divide, subtract and so on. Programs are not written in English but in a special language which the computer understands. Highly trained programmers write the programs.

The program is entered into the computer on a tape or disk. As the computer works, electricity flows through circuits which allow them to add, subtract, divide and multiply at extremely fast speeds. Once the work is done an answer appears on a screen or is printed on a tape, or paper.

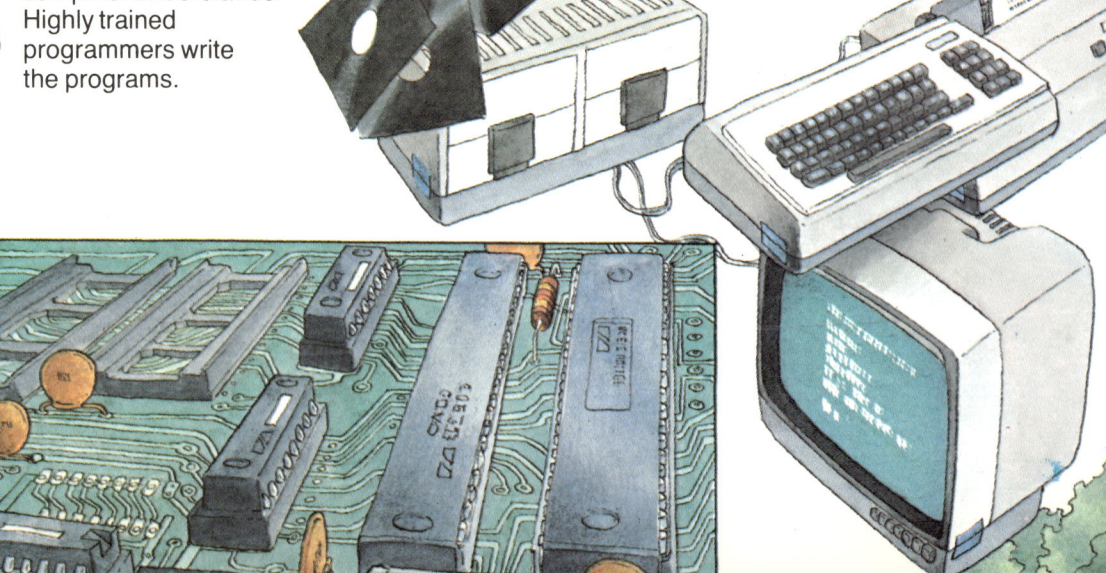

part of a computer circuit

52

Some machines, such as this harvester, can do a series of tasks at once without our attention, except for starting them. This machine cuts wheat, gathers it, separates the straw from the grain. Others do several tasks in sequence, such as washing machines, which wash, scrub, rinse and dry.

Raw Materials and Chemical Industries

Many raw materials such as coal, wood, iron and crude oil can be chemically changed into many new products. Take crude oil, for example. The black, sticky crude oil in the earth is pumped out of the ground and sent to either oil refineries or chemical plants. There it is changed into oil, gasoline and Vaseline, as well as numerous plastics, synthetic rubber and medicines. Many of the new products, like plastics, are shipped to factories to be made into finished products, such as toys and household items.

All through the process there are machines which help drill for the oil, pump it, and refine it; transport the chemicals; and make the plastic objects. There are machines to transport the objects to stores where they are sold.

the petroleum industry

Our age is called the Electronic Age. Computers, walkie-talkies, television sets are electronic devices. Turbines and generators in a nuclear power plant produce electricity, which is transmitted through wires to homes. Some electricity goes to television stations which send signals out into space. There, the signals are picked up by satellites. They send new signals back to earth thousands of miles from the original station to a TV dish which picks up the signals, makes them more powerful, and sends them out.

a nuclear power plant

The boy's television set picks them up so that he can watch his program, which was sent from thousands of miles away.

Science in Our Lives

Because of science we know a great deal about the world we live in. We know about the stars, the planets, dinosaurs, how plants and animals live and much, much more.

Science helps us answer many questions that interest us. How big is the sun? How smart are chimpanzees? What do germs look like? Scientists help us find answers.

To find answers, scientists perform experiments. They may, for example, mix chemicals together to see what happens.

Not all science is based on experiments. Astronomers search the skies for new information about planets and stars. Geologists may hunt for new rocks. But such searches give us more information about the world we live in.

Many scientists work for industries, trying to bring about technical progress. They want to produce things cheaper and faster.

Others work with medicines so that diseases can be cured. Many work in agriculture so that there will be more food for the hungry people of the world.

Because there is always a need for more scientists, many teach science to students.

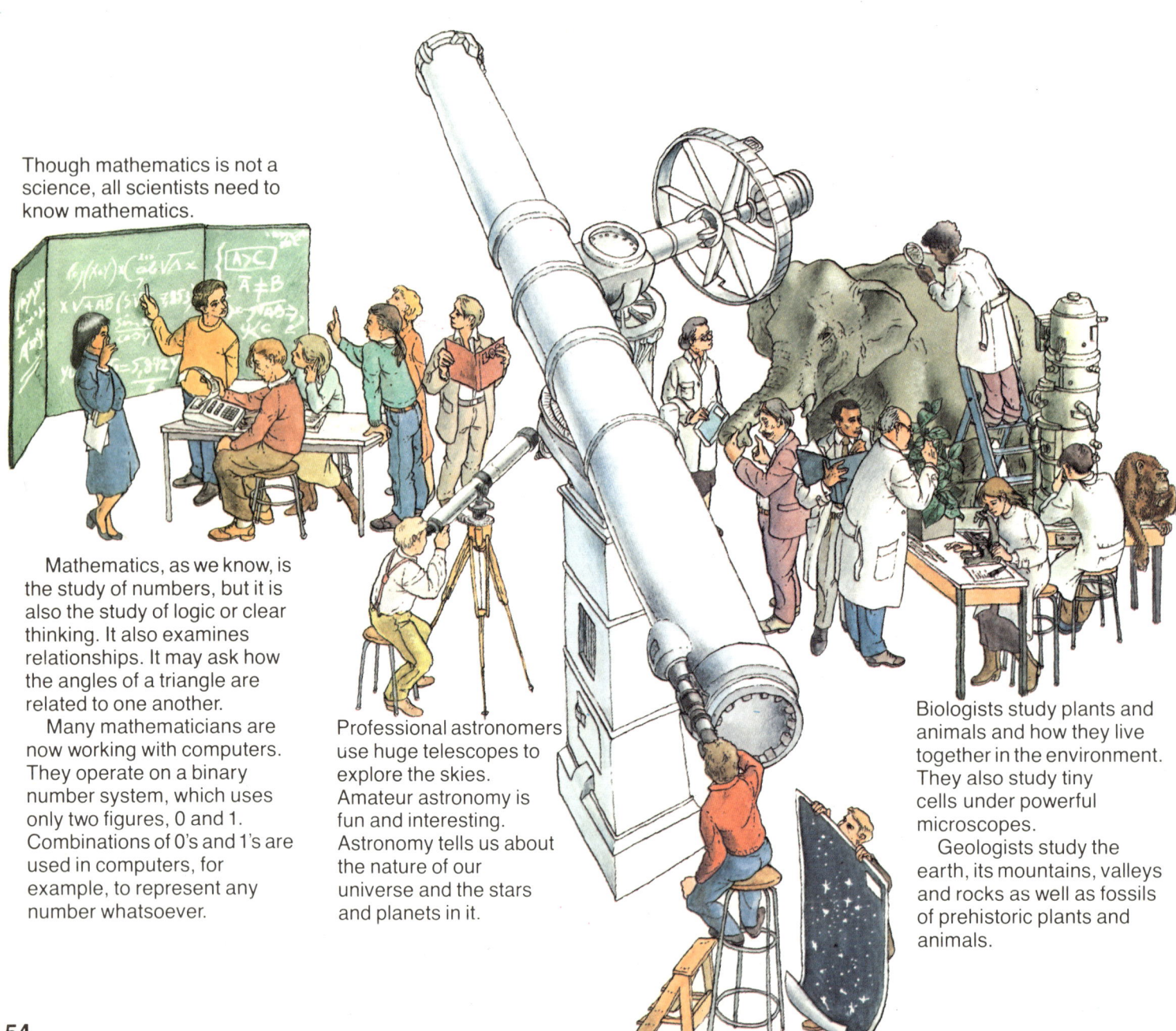

Though mathematics is not a science, all scientists need to know mathematics.

Mathematics, as we know, is the study of numbers, but it is also the study of logic or clear thinking. It also examines relationships. It may ask how the angles of a triangle are related to one another.

Many mathematicians are now working with computers. They operate on a binary number system, which uses only two figures, 0 and 1. Combinations of 0's and 1's are used in computers, for example, to represent any number whatsoever.

Professional astronomers use huge telescopes to explore the skies. Amateur astronomy is fun and interesting. Astronomy tells us about the nature of our universe and the stars and planets in it.

Biologists study plants and animals and how they live together in the environment. They also study tiny cells under powerful microscopes.

Geologists study the earth, its mountains, valleys and rocks as well as fossils of prehistoric plants and animals.

Physicists study mechanics, light, electricity, and the structure of the atom. They also work in many industries to make better television sets, computers and so on.

Chemists study what things are made of. They study minerals, hormones, and other chemicals to see how they are made. Using such information, they can make important chemicals: drugs, plastics, insecticides, and so on.

To understand chemicals better, they make models of their molecules to see what they look like.

Chemists often work with industries so various products, such as plastics, man-made fibers, paints and so on can be improved.

Economists study the production of goods: cars, shoes, steel, etc. They study the marketplace to see how goods are bought and sold. They also study taxes, banking and money. Psychologists study how the human mind works, so troubled people can be helped. They also study how people behave in groups. Sociologists study how people live in society and help plan better schools, get aid for the aged and so on. These scientists, more than others, work with people.

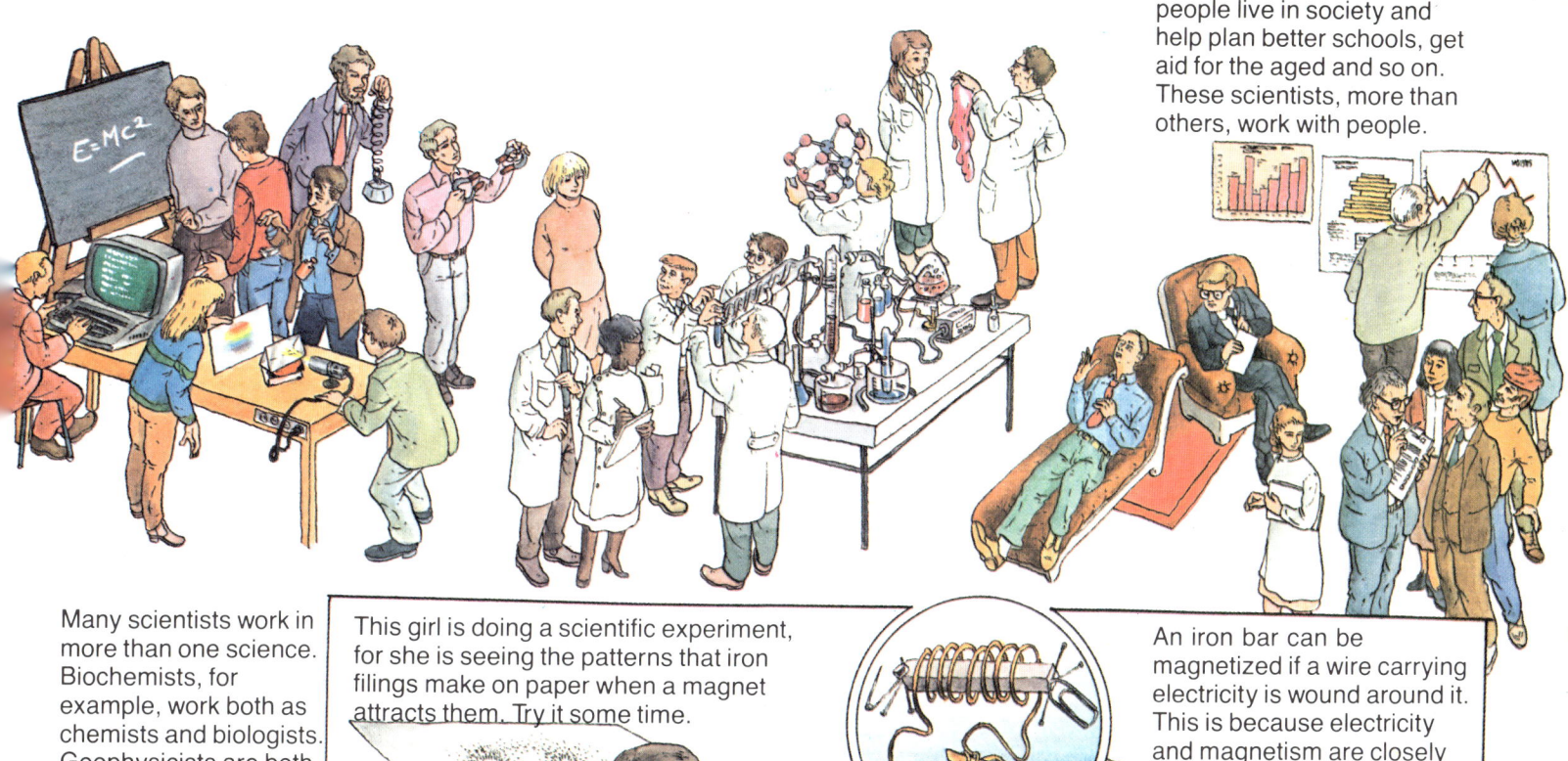

Many scientists work in more than one science. Biochemists, for example, work both as chemists and biologists. Geophysicists are both geologists and physicists.

This girl is doing a scientific experiment, for she is seeing the patterns that iron filings make on paper when a magnet attracts them. Try it some time.

An iron bar can be magnetized if a wire carrying electricity is wound around it. This is because electricity and magnetism are closely related.

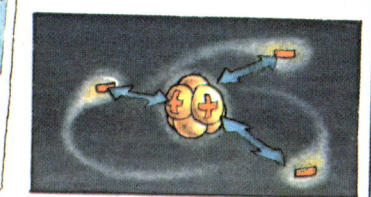

Inside an atom, a negative electron spins around one or more positive protons in the nucleus of the atom. The protons attract the electrons, somewhat in the same way the sun attracts the earth.

Magnetism is used in circuits of pinball machines.

The tape, in a tape recorder, is magnetized to record sounds.

The Arts

Singing and dancing seem natural. We also love to tell stories and draw pictures. That is what the arts are about—being creative, expressing ourselves in new and inventive ways.

We also need to admire, to marvel at something beautiful, perfect, and unusual, whether it is a song, book, painting or a performance.

Art communicates to others the emotions and thoughts of the artist. Artists always seem to find new languages with which to tell us how they see life, whether or not they were—or are—in harmony with the world, what they dream of, and what they desire.

Artists must work hard. They must know a great deal about techniques of their art and they must also study the works of others. Most of all they must practice their art, whether it is singing, dancing, painting, film, architecture, sculpture or writing.

These are professions. One must give one's whole life to one's art for it to succeed.

Many works of art made today will last for centuries, just as art of the past is still being admired today.

Drawing and painting are visual arts. Lines, shapes, and colors can be combined in many exciting ways.

We all enjoy looking at paintings and pictures. But what is most interesting is to learn how they are made, how to mix colors or place them together to get a certain effect, how to draw a portrait, landscape, or still life.

A sculptor works with clay, wood, metal, etc., to make three-dimensional forms. Architects design buildings and must think of how people will live in them. They must be well built, practical, and comfortable.

Photographers choose interesting subjects. They must present them in new and exciting ways. Film and television bring us news and entertainment. Each shot must be carefully planned so that the story moves forward in a natural and dramatic way.

Some artists work alone, such as painters, writers, sculptors. For some projects, such as making a movie, painting a mural, or designing buildings, many artists must work together and cooperate. A movie, for example, calls for many skilled people.

Music is the art of combining sounds. The voice and musical instruments make very different sounds, which create different effects depending on whether you listen to them one at a time or whether you hear a harmony made up of several notes. Composers write music and musicians play it.

Dancing is the most physical of the arts. Dancers must always exercise and keep their bodies trim. Many human emotions are expressed through dancing. Groups of dancers can form beautiful patterns on a stage.

Literature is the art of poets and writers who can express ideas and feelings by putting sentences on a page. When we read a book or hear one read to us, we can be transported to other times, other places. And the characters come alive.

In theatrical performances many arts come together: the playwright, who writes the play, musicians, stage designers, lighting experts, and of course the actors, dancers, and singers, who are often dressed in marvelous, colorful costumes which are made by designers.

Actors, musicians, and dancers perform in large halls for audiences. There is a give-and-take between the people on the stage and the audience which responds to them.

The arts reflect a civilization. The needs, desires, dreams, fears of all of us are mirrored in our arts. Twentieth-century art reflects our times. In a similar manner, ancient Greek or Chinese art reflected the thoughts and emotions of those peoples. Moreover, each civilization has changed the arts to suit its own needs. So it is that art changes from generation to generation.

57

Recreation

We all need to be restored, refreshed, and "re-created" — which is to say we need recreation. Without it our lives can become dull, boring and tiring.

Jigsaw puzzles, crossword puzzles, and so on stimulate us as we think. Many games such as chess and cards allow us to match wits with others. It is a lot of fun to watch an opponent and try to guess what he'll do if you make a certain move. It is exciting to outwit others, plan your strategy, and take risks as well.

To be good at a game requires a great deal of practice playing against others and meeting new challenges. In life we must meet challenges all the time. We must also solve puzzling problems. Childhood games give us practice in the skills that can help us later on.

Many childhood games and activities help us when we are older. In every game we play, we can learn something valuable, such as how to cooperate or compete fairly with others. This is one reason why so many people take games and sports so seriously, even while they are having fun.

There are so many different games. Some require only one person, others a team. Some use expensive equipment, such as computer games, others only a deck of cards or a few marbles. Some can be played at a desk; others need a large field to play on. Because of this variety, one can always find a game to play.

We all like to build things: cities out of blocks, good kites that fly high, and model airplanes. It is fun to use our hands and to see something we have actually made in motion.

The enjoyment of games lasts throughout life. Chess and card games give many adults hours and hours of pleasure. Often such games give adults a chance to get together on an evening after work. Or they can enjoy such games as crossword puzzles.

Sports are games which call for the use of your muscles as well as your brains.

Practicing a sport means breathing properly, having a body that is fit, limber, and coordinated. You also learn to use various sports equipment, such as skiis, mountain-climbing ropes, or sailboats.

Many sports call for team action. You must learn the rules of cooperation and good sportsmanship.

A true athlete knows the dangers of deep water, mountain cliffs, or high speed. He or she trains gradually, taking the advice of teachers who are more experienced and can guide a beginner's progress.

Many times families share in the enjoyment of sports —swimming, boating, skiing, bicycling, and horseback riding. Or they can enjoy more leisurely activities such as fishing from a boat or the banks of a stream. There is always some sport that grandparents, parents and children can enjoy together.

Everyone likes spectator sports, such as football, baseball, or horse racing. You can buy tickets and go to a stadium or watch the event on television.

Most spectator sports call for professional players, that is, those who receive money. Those who do not receive money or play for money, such as Olympic players, are called amateurs, even if some are better than professionals.

Sports events often bring people of different countries together. Though we may not know how to speak with others, because of language differences, we can always play games and sports with them. The most famous international games are the Olympics, held every four years, each time in a different country.

59

Communications

When you come home after school do you tell the family what you did that day? Do your brothers and sisters tell you what they did or saw?

If so, your family is communicating. Each person is sending information to the other.

There are many forms of communication. If you make a face at someone you are communicating. You send them information about your feelings. Speech is a form of communication, so is a letter, so is any writing.

Today there are huge worldwide communication systems that send information via telephone wires, radio waves, TV satellites across continents and the widest oceans.

In less than a second information is sent across the oceans. Because of this system we instantly get world news or speak to relatives in foreign lands.

Many new devices allow us to communicate in many different ways with the world we live in. Telephones, TV sets, tape cassettes, various computers, radios, and daily newspapers allow us to gather information in hundreds of different ways.

Today, new and better computers are available in schools, offices, and even in homes. Computers can be used in many ways. All can store a great deal of information in their memories. Soon interconnected computers drawing from many widely scattered individual computer memories will be able to obtain more information than that contained in the largest libraries. Researchers, office workers, and students will have all that information at their finger tips. Not only that—it will be instantaneously available.

By combining a television screen, a telephone, and a home computer, this information can appear on the screen.

You can also use a computer to keep track of bills, recipes and addresses. Special tapes contain lessons. You can learn Spanish, Chinese, world history or whatever you want. Computers are fun too. There are dozens of computer games to play.

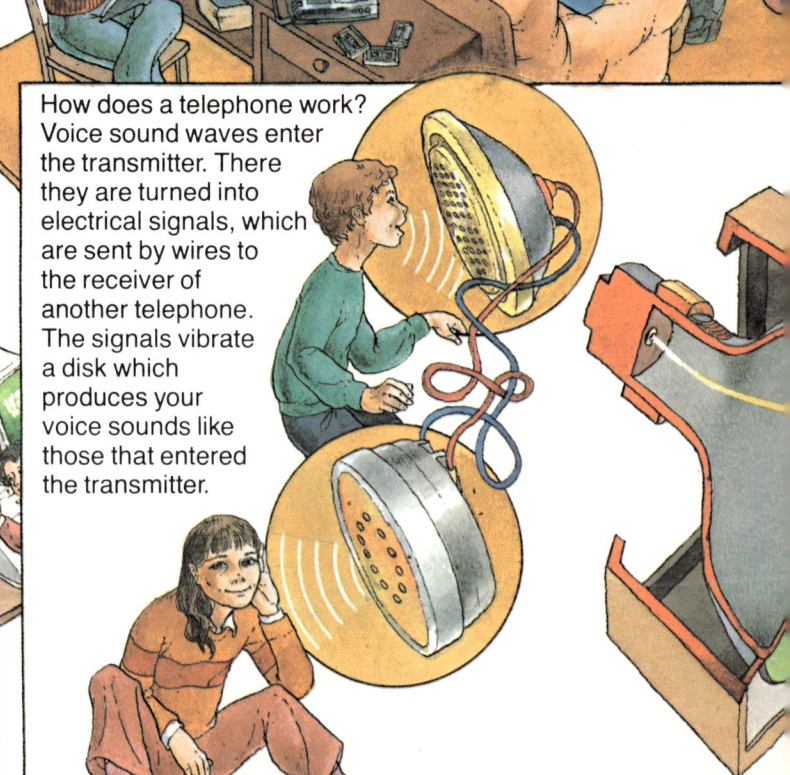

How does a telephone work? Voice sound waves enter the transmitter. There they are turned into electrical signals, which are sent by wires to the receiver of another telephone. The signals vibrate a disk which produces your voice sounds like those that entered the transmitter.

Several times a day we can get the news from radio, TV or newspapers. But where does the news come from and how does it really get to us? And, most important, who chooses what news we will receive?

News services have many correspondents all over the world. They are posted at key places: police stations, weather services, seats of government. When something important happens, they telephone to the service. It instantly sends messages to its subscribers: newspapers, TV or radio stations, which in turn give us the news.

TV can show us events as they occur on the sports field or battlefield, even if the event is taking place in a far-off land. We can actually see history being made.

Each issue of a newspaper and each TV and radio broadcast is the result of team work directed by an "editor in chief." He decides which news story should be emphasized and how much time or space to give to it. At newspaper offices, stories are written up as news is phoned in by reporters. The editor chooses among them. They are then typeset and printed.

Sometimes we can read about a news event within an hour of its happening. Thanks to a system of high-speed presses, and a network of delivery trucks, newspapers get to a newsstand very rapidly.

TV pictures are made when a stream of electrons hits a TV screen. They cause a dot on the screen to be either light or dark. These dots light up on a line and move very rapidly along it. There may be 600 to 800 lines on a screen.

Thirty times a second the lines, with their hundreds of thousands of dots, move across a screen so fast that our eyes see only a single picture.

Not all radios or TV sets are used for news or entertainment. Police radios direct police to crimes; radios direct ships and give them navigation information; airplanes keep in touch with airports by radio so that they know when they can land safely. Truckers and taxicab drivers and many other people also use radios. Many rural schools depend upon TV sets for classroom instructions.

Satellites in orbit around the earth can both receive and transmit TV and telephone signals. Because of this, they can relay signals sent from one continent to another and do it in a split second. They are an important link in a worldwide communications system.

61

Transportation

All of us must get from one place to another. To help us, there are transportation systems, which are big, complex, and very expensive. It may cost millions just to build a bridge across a river. But of course to do so, many construction problems must be met. Will floods tear the bridge away? Can it support the weight of trucks and cars? How will it actually be built? Engineers and workers face similar problems in building superhighways, tunnels, and in placing railroad tracks correctly to hold speeding trains. Highways must be constructed with safety in mind, without too many crossroads, where accidents are most likely to happen.

The flow of traffic on highways, railways, and in the air must be controlled. Highway signs tell motorists what to do. Police patrol the roads. Trains are controlled at rail yards. There, workers watch maps of the tracks for miles around. Electric signals show them where the trains are. They can also operate signals miles away, stopping and starting trains. Some signals on the tracks work automatically. Subways and undergrounds are controlled in much the same way for the safety of the millions of passengers who ride them every day.

Air traffic controllers keep track of airplanes landing and taking off via radar. They can see the airplanes on screens and can also speak directly to pilots over radios. The screens show when runways are clear and where other airplanes are located.

Motorists often need maps if they are in unfamiliar places so they know how to get where they are going. Map reading is a good skill to learn.

Many people love to travel to faraway places and see new things. Transportation allows quick and easy travel to most places on earth.

Subways or undergrounds help city travelers get to school or to offices every day. Because engines that burn oil would fill the tunnels with smoke, they must work by way of electric motors, which do not pollute the underground air.

On rivers and oceans many ships carry passengers, freight or petroleum products. Ferry boats carry people and cars short distances. They have regular schedules for departures and arrivals, as do most passenger and freight ships. Navigators keep track of the ship's course. They are helped by markers such as buoys, beacons, lighthouses, or guided by radio beams sent from land or satellites. In most large ports, they can get help from pilots who will steer the ship through the port to a wharf. Such pilots know all about the port where they work.

Tankers carrying oil or gasoline often hook up to hoses far offshore. These hoses and/or pipes carry the oil and gasoline to storage tanks onshore. They can also load up that way.

There are many kinds of boats and ships. Each is built for a special purpose. Sailboats are for pleasure; cruise ships for vacationers; tankers for oil; freighters for freight and sometimes a few passengers; river barges for freight.

When going long distances most people fly. Commercial airplanes take people and freight across continents and the widest oceans every day. Some, like the Concorde, are very fast, hitting speeds of about 1,000 mph. Passengers get on and off airplanes at large airports. Their baggage is checked and their passports may be stamped. Meals are served on the airplanes.

Seaplanes can land on water—seas, rivers, and lakes. They do not need an airfield. Many small towns have seaplane service.

In many ways, helicopters are the most interesting of all aircraft. Unlike the others, they can take off and land vertically. They can stop in midair and hover for long periods of time. Because of these remarkable abilities they can do many things other aircraft cannot do. They can, for example, pick up drowning people from a stormy sea. They can carry telephone poles into mountain regions and set them up correctly, in places where no trucks could ever get to. In a few places helicopters carry passengers. They take people from Wall Street in New York to airports outside of the city.

Hovercrafts glide above the surface of the water. Powerful fans compress the air beneath their hulls. This makes an "air cushion," which keeps them just above the water while propellers move them forward.

Blimps and balloons are lighter-than-air craft. Balloons are used for sport and blimps for patrolling coastlines or as floating billboards.

Submarines are warships. Today most are nuclear-powered and can stay under water for long periods of time.

63

The World of Tomorrow

No one knows for sure what the world of tomorrow will be like, except that it will be very different from our world. If present trends continue, we can say that there will be faster, more powerful computers. Robots capable of doing many types of work will be commonplace. Some will operate factory machines. Others will be household servants, picking up mail, washing dishes, dusting, etc. Various types of plants and animals will be produced by genetic engineering. Plants will provide medicinal drugs, special oils, and hardier food varieties that will grow farther north. The odd blue-and-white-striped pet may have been designed by scientists. Some animals may be designed to eat certain types of harmful insects, so that there will be no poisonous insecticides in the air.

People will still fall in love, like the couple in the picture. Grandmother may ride around in her own little helicopter. There will continue to be a family life. People will still cook meals. Committees will meet, people will have friends. So even though much will be different, many things will remain the same. Interestingly, some objects may not change: rolling pins, spoons and shoes. There are no aliens from other planets in the picture, for it is very unlikely that we will meet them —even if they may exist many, many light years away from us out in space. The people in the picture are wearing clothes similar to today's clothing, but a bit different, too. Perhaps we will learn to control the climate so the same sort of clothes can be worn all year long.

Why are there so many plants and trees in this vision of the future? Humans and all other animals will need them for the oxygen they give off into the atmosphere. Humans, even in the distant future, will have to preserve the earth's environment so that we can be here at all.

Some chimpanzees have been taught to speak in sign language. Scientists think that dolphins can communicate in a very complex language, which is unknown to us today. In the future, people may be able to talk with chimpanzees and dolphins. Imagine what we might be able to learn from them. They may know about many things which we do not know about. New genetically engineered animals may roam in the forests. Wild places of the earth may be quite different from those of today.

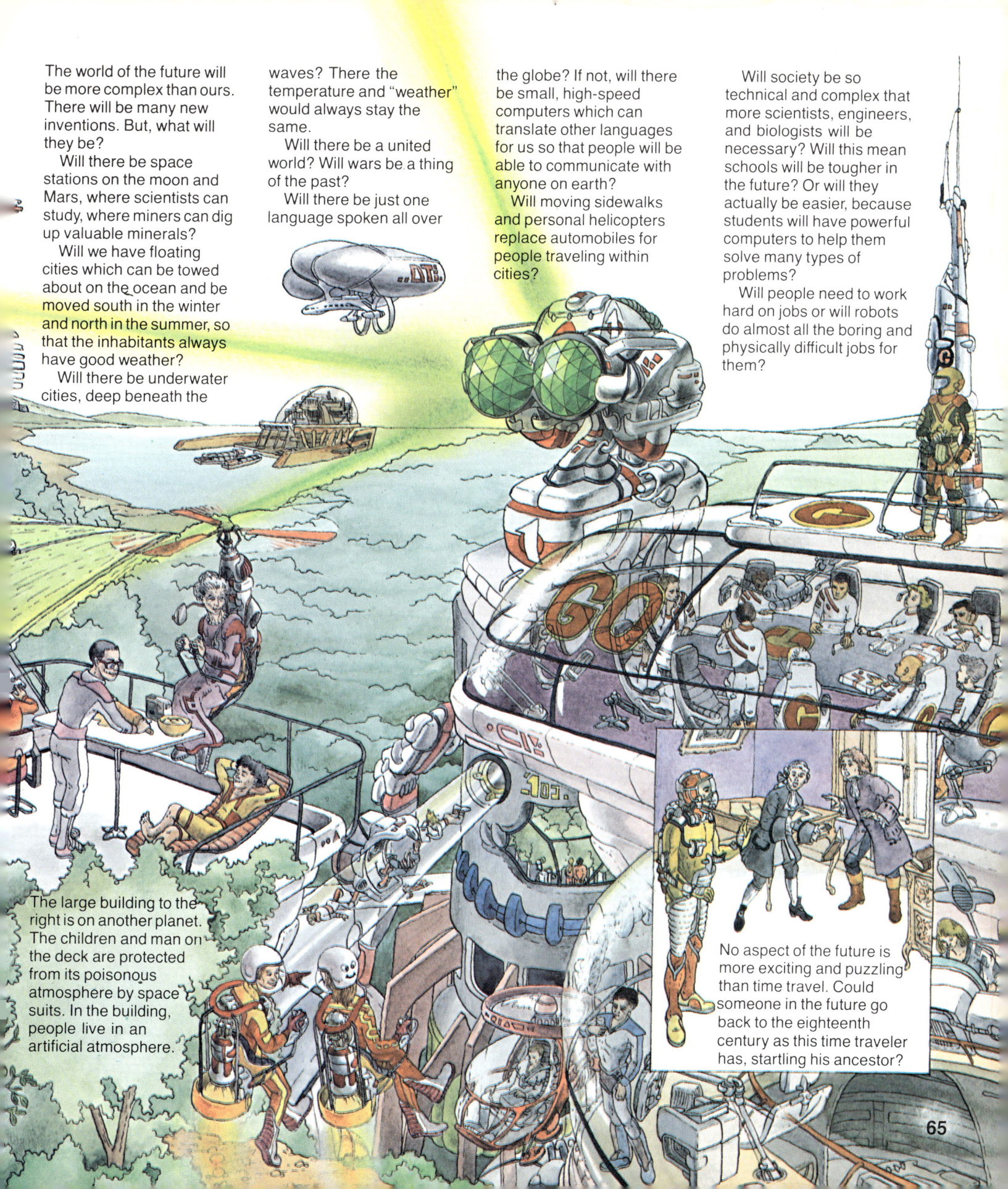

The world of the future will be more complex than ours. There will be many new inventions. But, what will they be?

Will there be space stations on the moon and Mars, where scientists can study, where miners can dig up valuable minerals?

Will we have floating cities which can be towed about on the ocean and be moved south in the winter and north in the summer, so that the inhabitants always have good weather?

Will there be underwater cities, deep beneath the waves? There the temperature and "weather" would always stay the same.

Will there be a united world? Will wars be a thing of the past?

Will there be just one language spoken all over the globe? If not, will there be small, high-speed computers which can translate other languages for us so that people will be able to communicate with anyone on earth?

Will moving sidewalks and personal helicopters replace automobiles for people traveling within cities?

Will society be so technical and complex that more scientists, engineers, and biologists will be necessary? Will this mean schools will be tougher in the future? Or will they actually be easier, because students will have powerful computers to help them solve many types of problems?

Will people need to work hard on jobs or will robots do almost all the boring and physically difficult jobs for them?

The large building to the right is on another planet. The children and man on the deck are protected from its poisonous atmosphere by space suits. In the building, people live in an artificial atmosphere.

No aspect of the future is more exciting and puzzling than time travel. Could someone in the future go back to the eighteenth century as this time traveler has, startling his ancestor?

65

Index

A

adobe houses, 46
aerial photography, 45
agave, 14
aging, 41
air (atmosphere), 26
airplanes, 63
air traffic controllers, 62
algae, 15
amethyst, 23
ammonite, 44
anemometer, 26
animal defenses, 18
animal territories, 18
annual plants, 13
Antarctic circumpolar current, 28
anthers, 12
antibodies, 40
apartment buildings, 47
arachnids, 16
archaeologists and their work, 45
architects, 56
armadillo, 18
arrowhead, 14
astronomy, 54
atoms, 11, 51

B

bacterium, 15
balance (ears), 39
balloons and blimps, 63
bark of trees, 14
barometer, 26, 27
bat, 19
bathyscaphe, 31
bay leaf, 13
bear, 19
bee, 9, 12, 16, 18
beech, 14
bee-eater, 18
belladonna (deadly nightshade), 15
biochemists, 55
biologists, 54
birch, 14
bird, 16
bird migration, 19
blood circulation, 35
blood corpuscles, 11
bones of the skeleton, 36
borage, 13
brain, 38
brain neuron cells, 11
bricks, 47
bulb, 13
butterfly, 18
butterfly metamorphosis, 17

C

calcite, 23
calculators, 52
calories, 34
cambium of spring and fall, 14
canals, 30
carbon, 10
carniverous plant, 15
castor bean, 13
caterpillar, 17
cave dwellings, 46
cells, cell division, 11
cereals, 13
chameleon, 18
chanterelle mushroom, 15
cheetah, 19
chemists, 54, 55
chestnut, 14
chicken reproduction, 17
chimpanzees, 64
chlorophyll in leaf cells, 15
chrysalis or pupa, 17
circulation of air around the earth, 26
city life, 48, 49
clothing for the future, 64
clouds, 26
coffee, 13
colchicum (crocus), 15
cold-blooded animals, 32
compass, 30
computers, 52, 54, 60
computer language, 52, 54
continents, how they were formed, 23
copper, 23
cotton, 13
cotyledon, 12
crayfish, 18
crocodile, 18

D

dams, 30
dancers, 57
death cup mushroom, 15
deer, 18
diamond, 23
digitalis (foxglove), 15
dinosaur, 45
diseases, 40
dolphins, 64
dormouse, 19

E

eagle, 18
earth's crust, mantle, core, 22
earthworm, 16
ecology, 9
economists, 55
electricity, 51, 53
electrons, 11, 51
elements, 10
emerald, 23
energy sources, 50
environment, 8
environmental protection, 21
eucalyptus, 14, 15
explorations in outer space, 21, 24

F

fabrics, 13
fern spores, 15
fertilization of seeds, 12
fetus, 42, 43
fire, 33
fish, 16
flax, 13
fly agaric mushroom, 15
frog reproduction, 17
fruits, 13
future, some speculations, 65

G

galaxies, 25
games, 58
gasoline engine, 50
geese, 19
geologists, 54
geophysicists, 55
gills, gill slits of fish, 16
glacier, 23, 29
glands, 41
gold, 23
golden hamster, 18
graphite, 22
Gulf Stream, 28
gypsies, 47
gypsum, 22

H

harvester, 53
healing, in humans, 40
hearing (ears), 38
heart, 35
heart muscles, 37
heartwood, 14
helicopters, 63
herbs, culinary, 13
hibernation of animals, 19
highways, 62
holly, 14
Homo sapiens sapiens, 44
hormones, 41
houseboats (barges, junks), 47
hovercraft, 63
human birth, 43
human circulation, 34
human conception, 42
human digestion, 34
human evolution, 44
human food needs, 34
human growth, 43
human nervous system, 36, 37
human reproduction, 42
human respiratory system, 34, 35
human sexual development, 43
humans transforming nature, 20
hydrogen, 10
hygrometer, 26
hypholoma mushroom, 15

I

insects, 9, 16
insect reproduction, 17
insulation to keep heat in or out, 33

invertebrate animals, 16
involuntary muscles, 37
ivy, 14

J

joints in human body, 36
jute, 13

L

lakes, 29
laurel, 14
lava, 22
leaf, cross section, 15
leaves, 14
life cycle, 10
life on another planet, 65
limestone, 22, 29
locusts, 19
log cabins, 46
loggerhead turtle, 19
lungs, 35

M

machines, 52
magma of volcano, 22
magnetism, 55
magpie, 18
mallard ducks, 19
mammal, 16
mammal reproduction, 17
mammoth, 44
mangrove, 14
map reading, 62
mathematics, 54
meadow mushroom, 15
medicinal plants, 13
menstruation, 42
meteors, 26
Mid-Atlantic Ridge, 28
Milky Way, 22
minerals under the sea, 31
mistletoe, 15
mole, 18
molecules, 11
mollusks, 16
moon, 21, 24, 25
mosses, 15
mountain ash, 14
mountains, how they were formed, 23
mulberry, 14
muscles in human body, 36
musicians, 57
mycelium, 15

N

natural gas, 51
neutron, 11
newspapers, 61
news services, radio, TV, newspapers, 61
nomads, 47
nuclear power, 51, 53
nucleus of the atom, 11

O

oak, 14
oceans, 28
olive, 13, 14
Olympic games, 59
orbit and rotation of the earth, 25
osprey, 19
ovary, 12
ovule, 12
oxygen in atmosphere, 26
oxygen in human respiration, 34, 35

P

painters, 56
parsley, 13
perennial plants, 13
petroleum industry, 53
pheasant, 18
philiota mushroom, 15
photographers, 56
physicists, 55
pine, 14
pistil, 12
planets, 24
plankton, 28
plants and trees for oxygen, 64
pollen, 12
Pompeii, 45
poplar, 14
poppy, 13
porcupine, 18
praying mantis, 18
prehistory, 44
preserving food, canning, freezing, 33
protons, 11
psychologists, 55

Q

quartz, 23

R

radio telescopes, 24
raffia, 14
rain, 27
reproduction, 17
rhinoceros, 18
rhizome, 13
rivers, 29
robin, 18
robots, 64
root, 13

S

salmon migration, 19
salt basins, 31
sandstone, 22
sap, crude and enriched, 14
satellites for worldwide communication, 61
scorpion, 16
scrub oak, 14
sculptors, 56
sea farms for fish and shellfish, 31
seaplanes, 63
seaweed, 15, 30
seeds, 13
shale, 22
shellfish, 16
ships and boats, 63
sight (eyes), 38
skeleton in human body, 36
smell (nostrils), 39
snail, 16
sociologists, 55
solar energy, 51
solar system, formation, 22
sonar, 30, 31
spices, 13
spiders, 16
spinal column in humans, 37
sports, 59
stars, 25
steam engine, 50
stomata of leaves, 15
storms, 27
submarines, 63
subways, 62
summer, 32
sun, 24, 25
sunlight, 10
swallows, 19

T

tadpole, 17
tarragon, 13

taste (tongue), 39
teepees, 46
teeth, 41
telephone, 60
television, 53, 61
tents, 47
theater, 57
thermometer, 26, 32
thermos (vacuum) bottles, 33
thyme, 13
tides, 28
tiger, 18
time travel, 65
time zones, 25
tool making, 20
tornado, 27
touch (skin), 39
trains, 62
trawlers for fish, 30
tree bud, 14
trees, 14, 15
tuber, 13
turbines, 50
turtle, 18

U

undersea craft, 31

V

vaccines, 40
vegetables, 13
Venus's-flytrap, 15
vertebrate animals, 16
vitamins, 34
voice (vocal cords), 39
volcanoes, 22
volcanoes under the sea, 28

W

walnut, 14
warm-blooded animals, 32
water, 11
waves, 28
weather balloons, 27
weather reports, 27
whale, 19, 31
wild boar, 18
willow, 14
windmill for electricity, 50
wind sock, 27
winter, 32
woodchuck, 19

woodpecker, 18
wren, 18
writers, 57

Y

yellow boletus mushroom, 15

Z

zebra, 17